Let's Be
Realistic
About Your
Church Budget

Let's Be Realistic

About Your
Church Budget

Douglas W. Johnson

Judson Press® Valley Forge

LET'S BE REALISTIC ABOUT YOUR CHURCH BUDGET
Copyright © 1984
Judson Press, Valley Forge, PA 19482-0851

Library of Congress Cataloging in Publication Data

Johnson, Douglas W., 1934–
  Let's be realistic about your church budget.

  Bibliography: p.
  1. Church finance. I. Title.
BV770.J59 1984   254.8   83-17539
ISBN 0-8170-1025-4

The name JUDSON PRESS is registered as a trademark in the U.S. Patent Office. Printed in the U.S.A. ⊕

This book is dedicated to my parents.

Contents

Preface

An old man said to me when I was quite young, "Son, you have a lot of ideas. Someday I hope you come back down to earth and live with the rest of us." The old man was asking for realism to temper whatever we plan so that those dreams we have can be put into practice.

Since he said it, many others have commented, "So we have a plan. What next?" This book seeks to help answer that question. The learnings in it have come from experience, study, and observation. They are presented as guides for your study and use. You may have to adapt the material for your situation, but what is presented does work.

I am grateful to the people whose patience over the years has helped keep realism as a major part of my planning. I trust their legacy has been transmitted as carefully as they taught it to me.

Douglas W. Johnson
Ridgewood, New Jersey

1

Realism in the Plan

That was one of the best planning retreats we've ever had. I'm very excited about the program possibilities for next year."

"You took the words right out of my mouth, Helen. We've got the momentum! Now we know where we're going as a congregation."

"I'm glad to hear you say that, George. If the plan is going to be carried out, you two plus a lot of others are going to have to be very enthusiastic and work very hard."

As an aside in a lowered voice the pastor said, "And it's going to take a lot of my time trying to convince John that what we're doing is affordable." The three of them laughed as they parted.

The next morning the pastor received a call from John. Apparently the treasurer had some reservations about the feasibility of the plans that had come out of the planning retreat.

"Good to hear from you, John. I hope you felt as good about our planning session as I did," the pastor said cautiously.

"It was a good session, Pastor. We got a fix on direction and did a lot of talking about programs. If we try hard, we might even get one or two under way."

"It will take a lot of work but I hope we can do more than one or two programs. Don't you think we can do more than two?"

"Well, when you come right down to it, Pastor, I'm not sure we can do anything more than we're doing right now. We're having a dickens of a time meeting current expenses."

"That's the reason we plan. We want to give people a new concept of what the church can do . . . what the ministry of the church is all about. A new vision will give them some excitement and they will be more willing to support new programs."

"You pastors all have the same theory. It's good to get people excited and all that but it takes hard cash to run the show. I'm not trying to throw cold water on your plans, Pastor, but something has to be done to connect those plans to income. We have to pay for what we do."

"But we have a program budget! Everything is connected to a dollar figure. We know where the money is going. If we don't have enough for a program, it doesn't get started."

"I know that, Pastor. Program budgets are all right for some organizations with predictable income. In those organizations programs can be cut if they aren't working out. But the church is different. The church has to have a worship service even if it isn't economically feasible. We need a pastor even if there is barely enough money to pay the fuel bill. You see, Pastor, what the church stands for requires certain things. After these things are paid for, then we can talk about new programs."

"But we aren't going to begin everything right away. Our plan calls for phasing in programs over three or four years. We ought to be able to do that."

"If you're talking logic, I agree. But the church isn't that easy to change, Pastor. People have to know that certain things are going to be done before they're going to get serious about change. You're not going to get any place if all you do is talk about a plan."

The pastor, as might be expected, was upset with this conversation. He felt that the treasurer, who had a great deal of influence in the congregation, was being difficult. The pastor was extremely frustrated.

At least four issues are raised by this conversation. These are: the differences between hopes and obligations, fixed and discretionary expenses, possibilities and needs, and the new and the old. The conversation illustrates the difference between developing a plan and being realistic enough to get that plan implemented by a congregation.

Raising Hopes by Planning Versus the Realism of Obligations

The planning process is designed to be a thoughtful, exciting experience. It assists groups to remember their reason for being and the history of how they got to where they are currently. This process also includes an analysis of the persons involved and the situation in which they find themselves. The final step in the planning process is plotting a means for moving into the future.

One inherent danger of such a process is the temptation to return to some golden yesterday by applying a "quick fix," e.g., "All we need is more young people," to current activities. This solution might come out of a planning session but it must be based on a thorough analysis of potentials rather than on a strictly emotional desire for such a change.

Another danger in planning is that people begin to feel that all they have to do is put the plan together. Nothing is further from the truth. Planning is creating a way to approach an organization's future. It is not necessarily the way in which the organization will ultimately function. Also, much work comes between the planning and the realization of that planning.

Yet another danger of the planning process is that an analysis of the present and the past of an organization may result in a negative outlook. When a congregation has not done well, statistics can compound an already-present feeling of failure. When this happens, the planning process can turn into a "downer," rather than being uplifting and future oriented.

In spite of these dangers, the usual result of a good planning experience is enthusiasm and a desire to get started with the future right now! The group whose conversation was recorded at the start of this chapter was at that point. Group members had just finished their retreat and had much hope in what they could and should be doing. Enthusiasm came from their joint decisions and from the commitment which attends planning meetings. Hope was there but so was the hidden part of planning: obligations. It was to these that the treasurer pointed in the conversation with the pastor.

A plan is future oriented. However, a plan which is realistic also takes into consideration the present and its opportunities and burdens as well as future possibilities. Unfortunately, many people who attend planning retreats often focus only on the future. It becomes necessary, therefore, for some member of the planning group to raise the question of obligations.

The treasurer was the self-appointed person in this congregation to say, "How can we get from where we are now to the plan?" The answer or lack of an answer to this question has scuttled the hopes raised by many a planning retreat. Often mechanisms for accomplishing a plan have not worked well and the plan has been slowly abandoned.

If a congregation wants to move from hopes to actuality it must consider carefully current and future obligations as a part of the plan. People often forget that current obligations will not suddenly be wiped out by a new plan. Obligations can be changed but the change takes place slowly.

Congregational obligations are both physical and spiritual. Physical obligations include maintenance of a facility so that people may use it for worship, education, fellowship, and service activities. The facility must be safe, temperate, clean, in good repair, and attractive. The roof can't be allowed to leak, the furnace and/or air conditioning must work properly, stairs must be sturdy, carpets should be clean, windows should be sealed and not cracked, and so forth. The general category of physical obligations must be divided into very specific needs if a congregation is to understand fully the costs of keeping a place of meeting open and functioning.

Other physical obligations may include a parsonage, a parking lot, sidewalks, and any other aspect of the environment which a congregation uses and for which it has responsibility.

One part of a plan might be to reduce the physical obligations by sharing a meeting place with another congregation. However, a congregation can never fully eliminate these obligations since there are physical maintenance obligations no matter where a group meets.

Spiritual obligations include caring for the worship needs of shut-ins, providing educational and devotional materials for members and nonmembers, training leaders and teachers for all parts of the congregation's program including the church school, providing hymnals and music for the congregation and the choir, planning and conducting worship services, and maintaining the office equipment and supplies which are used to communicate with the membership and outside communities. While these are generally included in budget costs, they often are overlooked in planning meetings because they are ever-present obligations rather than being future oriented.

Yet these constant spiritual and educational activities of a congregation cost money and time. They detract from resources which are available for a new future. That is the reason the treasurer was less than optimistic about the plans which were formulated in the planning retreat. The treasurer was really saying that if the congregation intended to provide the present level of services to the members and to the community, it would be difficult to do much else. He was bringing their hopes down to earth with the realism of obligations.

Discretionary and Fixed Expenses

In his argument for a realistic outlook, the treasurer pointed out the difference between fixed and discretionary expenses. All budgets have these two components. Fixed expenses are long-term and require regular payment of a certain amount each month, quarter, or year. Fixed expenses must be met before any other bills are paid.

One category of fixed expenses is physical facilities. For most congregations these include electricity, fuel, maintenance, mortgage payments, and the like. While each congregation may have a different mix of fixed expenses, the common characteristic of such obligations is that they must be paid or the congregation faces curtailment of needed services.

A second category of fixed expenses is pastoral leadership. When a pastor is added to a congregation's budget, the number of fixed expenses increases. Fixed expenses for pastoral services include contributions to the pastor's pension, insurance, phone, continuing education, salary, and travel. The cost of each of these may vary from year to year but once a pastor is called to a congregation, expenses related to that position become fixed. It is possible to curtail these expenses but this results in a limitation of pastoral services.

A third category of fixed expenses relates to the denomination of which a church is a member. While such expenses for many congregations may seem to be less than obligatory, the denomination is a primary conduit for congregations to express their national and world mission outreach. Congregations send money to national agencies and world mission stations through the denomination. They also send money to support the denomination's administrative and program operations.

The congregation may decide to which specific missions it sends its money. However, a denominational formula may request a specific amount for national and world missions each year from a congregation. Since the congregation is a part of the denomination, these amounts become fixed expenses.

The second major division of a budget is discretionary expenses, those over which a congregation has more immediate control. Discretionary expenses include music, janitorial services, staff additions, church school supplies, program-related items, as well as increases in salaries and benefits for the present staff. These are the kinds of expenses a church can cut back or expand without immediately affecting the existence of the congregation.

An example of a discretionary expense is that of giving a Bible to each member of a teenage church school class. This is a useful but not necessary expense. Other illustrations are the salary for a secretary which a congregation decides to hire rather than relying on volunteers; the expenses involved in hiring a music director or organist rather than depending on volunteers. These are changes in procedure. Work may be done better and more efficiently, but the essential functioning of the congregation is not at stake.

Money which is not used for fixed expenses can be used for any purpose decided upon by the governing body of the congregation. This group might decide to put a percentage of its income into a permanent reserve fund, the amount of which can be increased by annual decision. The congregation decides how much is going into the account and some years may decide not to put anything into it at all.

The ratio of fixed expenses to discretionary expenses changes in time. Some church leaders feel that it is important always to have large fixed expenses related to the building because members can see it as a place they are helping to build. These leaders believe that people will contribute to the building because it signifies success. Not only that, it is a symbol people in the community recognize. It has community stature and tells something about the people who use it. Some congregations seem to thrive on this method of maintaining enthusiasm.

Another group of church leaders may feel that most of a congregation's money should be used for program purposes. Their emphasis is to free as much money as possible from fixed expenses and make the budget include mostly discretionary expenses. Many such congregations do well for a time but change their program emphases frequently. There seems to be a lack of long-term commitment to their own history and some feeling of rootlessness within the congregation.

People need psychologically to feel that they are building something for themselves. This means money must be spent on symbols to hold groups together. Programs are not as powerful in doing that over the long term as is a building. Even the Sunday church school class which has been around for years must have its own place to meet. A part of its identity is the facility.

The treasurer was pointing out the difference in these two types of expenses to the pastor. While the pastor may have recognized the difference between the types of expenses, he did not appreciate their significance for planning. The pastor felt that fixed expenses could be changed merely by deciding not to use the money for those items. The treasurer underscored the feeling of the congregation, namely, "We are anxious to do new things but only as add-ons to what we're already doing."

No matter how a congregation views its budget, it takes time to change the precentages of fixed and discretionary expenses. The reason is clear. Fixed expenses are long-term obligations. For example, a mortgage lasts for twenty to thirty years.

Pastoral leadership is another fixed expense which takes time to change. A pastor is a symbol to the community about the kind of group he or she represents. The pastor authenticates the message and concern of the group in the community. While the pastor as a person changes, the position is critical to the long-term life of the congregation. The symbol doesn't change.

A congregation wanting to change its fixed expenses must deal with its place and stature in the community, its self-image as a congregation, and its purposes. Money is not the issue so much as are the history and expectations of the congregation.

This doesn't mean change isn't possible or shouldn't be attempted. Changes in the ratio of fixed to discretionary expenses by a congregation can be achieved when it agrees that its current image needs to be changed to fit more nearly its feelings of commitment to Christ. The whole congregation must undergo the change, not just the budget committee.

It was this need to consider the deeper issue of "what we're all about as a congregation" that prompted the treasurer's call to the pastor. The pastor's enthusiasm seemed to be clouding his view of reality. On the other hand, the pastor was frustrated because at the planning retreat new areas of service had been discovered and yet the treasurer seemed unwilling to work at instituting change. Those who have felt the tensions between reality and the plans made in a splendid planning retreat know the degree of frustration which can be kindled.

"It's great to have these new programs, Pastor, but we have to have some place to hold them. That's going to cost more money than we have available." These are not words to throw cold water on a pastor. They are a challenge. It is up to the pastor to bring the plan and current operations into healthy tension. This is the way a pastor can lead a congregation into long-term change and capitalize on the hopes created during the planning process.

This points to another reality in the planning and implementation process: acquiring the ability to state clearly what are long-range possibilities as opposed to immediate needs.

Long-Term Possibilities Versus Immediate Needs

Let's go back to the pastor's conversation with the two lay persons. The pastor let them know that he expected the plan to be implemented immediately. He was asking their help in the implementation process. His comment about having to convince the treasurer to go along with the plan was the only indication that it might not be possible to implement it tomorrow. Nothing in his conversation suggested to the lay persons a time schedule which would bring the plan into action over time. Only when the treasurer called did he mention long-term phase-ins of new programs.

The pastor's enthusiasm got in the way of rational planning. A planning retreat stretches minds and participants often feel change is imminent. When the new era doesn't begin right away they become confused, disappointed, angry, and disillusioned, generally in that order. They have difficulty because the process did not make clear that many of the plans are long range, that is, they will be phased in over two to four years rather than immediately. This one little oversight creates many of the problems associated with long-range planning.

That was a mistake the pastor began to regret later. Only after the treasurer called was the pastor aware of the consequences of the oversight. How crucial was this mistake? An illustration using the family budget gives a clue to the seriousness of this oversight.

In the family, immediate needs include food, clothing, shelter, and transportation. These are requirements which must be met *now* and in the future. The family can't function without them.

On the other hand, owning a home, buying a new automobile, taking a vacation, or putting money into savings are long-range possibilities. They are not essential now but can become a part of the life-style of the family over the years. The family has to survive in the present before it can begin to achieve goals for the future.

A plan and a budget must include both needs and possibilities if they are to assure the future. A church, like a family, has immediate needs, primarily the fixed expenses discussed previously, as well as long-term hopes. The hopes may be to add another staff member, to buy more hymnals, to refurbish the building, to add a parking lot, or to purchase and install a good sound system. These may seem like necessities but, in the experience of most congregations, they are not essential to continued existence. They are long-term possibilities.

Suppose a congregation devises a plan to develop a program for single adults. The plan allocates two thousand dollars to hire a coordinator and pay for supplies to get the program started. The treasurer tells the pastor that due to a change in the utility bill, the two thousand dollars will not be available this year. The result can be to cut the single adult program out of the budget. If this happens, a discretionary expense has been denied because of an increase in a fixed expense. In many situations this is exactly what would happen, and what would cause widespread discouragement and a feeling that planning isn't worthwhile.

To prevent the cancellation of a possible program because of a fixed expense, a congregation's plan must be constructed to

separate immediate need from long-term possibilities. What are
the needs in the projected single adult program? A need for the
congregation, if it is to act on its purposes, is to begin a single
adult program. A need for the budget is to meet the fixed
expenses. A need for the pastor is to assist the congregation to
fulfill its purposes. A need for the treasurer is to make certain
the congregation remains fiscally solvent and responsible. All
of these needs must be met in the immediate *now* if the plan is
going to succeed. Therefore, it becomes necessary to decide how
a single adult ministry can become reality.

What must this congregation do right now if it is to begin the
program? (See *The Challenge of Single Adult Ministry,* Judson Press,
1982, for a more complete description.) First of all, the sum of
two thousand dollars is not needed if volunteers do the background work required to determine the feasibility of the new
program. Second, enough money to do the groundwork for the
program—for example, sending the announcements and letters—can be allocated from other budget items. Third, money
for the program can be included in the budgets for a year or
two hence. It takes nearly a year to complete the groundwork
before a program can be fully instituted. Volunteers and limited
expenditures may be used in the meantime. Fourth, such a
program can be a pay-as-you-go operation, with funds coming
from small entrance fees to programs or from special collections.

The immediate need, in this illustration, is to find one or more
capable volunteers to help design and initiate the program. The
pastor can oversee these persons for at least eighteen months.
As a consequence, the immediate needs cited here can be met
and the program can begin.

The long-range possibilities can be investigated at the same
time the groundwork for the program is being done. For instance, the governing body and the pastor can work out ways
to find new money for the program. Long-term possibilities
include hiring a part-time or full-time director, providing money
for advertising in newspapers and in the media, having someone
be a full sponsor rather than asking persons merely to contribute
to the program, and preparing separate facilities for a meeting
room. These are not needs but enhancements in the life-style
of the group. They aren't needed until the group is formed and
is meeting.

This illustration indicates that planning must include a process which can separate immediate needs from long-term possibilities. Each program of a congregation contains both elements and a realistic plan takes account of both. The plan must assign various developmental stages and program enhancements to specific budget years.

One congregation, considering adding a part-time music director for children, put the cost for this position in a budget three years into the future. Members then designed an escalating program for children's music to build up to the time when a director would be needed. Their intent in the plan and budget was to create and evaluate a program need.

Over the three-year period they used volunteers and the current music director. Their strategy allowed them time to develop the program using existing resources and to evaluate its progress before becoming committed to a need. They gave themselves time and were realistic in their expectations.

A plan ought to contain this kind of implementation process. It should outline programs which a congregation ought to have to meet its purposes and specify a date by which the programs should be implemented. Subsequent budgets will reflect these phase-ins. Meanwhile the congregation does what it can with current resources.

While this is a logical sequence that works, people are often impatient. They want to get everything started immediately. Some people even threaten to leave when a congregation seems to be too slow in implementing their pet programs. Congregations can ill afford to lose members, especially active members. On the other hand, it is better to spend time with disgruntled members who are impatient with the slowness of program development than it is to try to restore trust after a program has been dropped because of a lack of funds. People can be guided into constructive activities to help develop programs so they will not leave. (See *The Care and Feeding of Volunteers*, Abingdon Press, 1978, for a more complete discussion of this subject.) But it takes a long time to win back those persons who become disillusioned when a program fails. (See *Reaching Out to the Unchurched*, Judson Press, 1983, for a more complete discussion.)

A part of every planning session must include a time for separating immediate needs from long-term possibilities in the same way that fixed and discretionary expenses are identified. This may come at the conclusion of the session or it may be a requirement imposed on all programs as they are designed. The emphasis is not on keeping the budget down or cutting back on program. The emphasis is upon building realistic expectations and scheduling expansion and improvement into the plan. Not only will the programs be designed better and in more detail, but the crunch between fixed and discretionary expenses will be lessened. The plan will have a sense of probability about it that makes it workable.

A planning process must raise hopes. If it doesn't, it hasn't been done correctly. Yet the process must aim at implementation on a schedule which is realistic and within the capabilities of the congregation. This means making compromises. The compromises will be on process and techniques, not on quality or end results.

Enthusiasm for the New Versus Working Well with the Old

A fourth issue raised by the conversation between the pastor and the two lay persons is created by the enthusiasm they had for new ideas and program possibilities. In the same way that the treasurer had to raise the obligation questions, someone will need to remind the planners that it is necessary to take into account how well the present programs are moving along as well as look at new programs and ideas. Change, to be effective, builds on the present. Herein lies a problem.

Newness generates enthusiasm and hope. "We ought to try it. It could give us a real boost!" is the way one church leader reacted when confronted with a new but totally inappropriate (for her congregation) way of visitation evangelism.

The lure of the new is a powerful incentive for getting some church leaders to think about change. Every new technique for getting people to come through the doors of the church is latched onto as if it were a preordained "fixit" for the congregation. Most congregations find, after they have tried several surefire techniques for church growth, that the new doesn't necessarily work for them.

A congregation must pick and choose among the various ideas and techniques for improving ministry in order to find the one it can use best. Even then it must test and modify it through experience. Enthusiasm must be tempered with an appreciation of the good things happening now.

A planning session needs to introduce new concepts, give people opportunities to look at the church and its present programs in different ways, and provide the incentive to think through new possibilities for the congregation. These are essential ingredients for a successful planning session. This is the process which generates the enthusiasm. But the work has not really begun. It becomes an effort not to lose that enthusiasm as the congregation develops its strategies for implementation.

It is this process of bringing the new into juxtaposition with existing programs and procedures that spells the difference between the success or failure of a plan. A good plan may cause a spirit of euphoria but this is meaningless in the long run unless a solid foundation for moving into the future is established.

"We always come out of the planning retreat full of excitement. Then about a month later we're swallowed up by budget problems and trying to keep the current program moving. Maybe we need that annual session as a shot in the arm. I don't know. But let me tell you, after a few years it's discouraging. Planning doesn't seem to make any difference in the way things go around here."

This woman wasn't able to conceal her underlying frustration. The members of her congregation had enthusiasm but did not build on the foundation of current programs in order to get some of the new concepts from the planning session into the operations of the congregation. Compare her sense of defeat with a similar feeling from a lay person from a congregation with an exactly opposite procedure of innovation.

"Our annual planning session is a kind of private nightmare for me. We go into it and are bombarded with new ideas, techniques, and possibilities. We don't do a lot of evaluation. We assume someone knows how the church is running. We sit there and cut out programs and put new ones in their places. Sometimes there doesn't seem to be any apparent reason for our decisions.

"For example, we decided to cut out our training program for church school volunteers this year and make available to them training tapes to take home. Well, I'm active in the church school and I'll tell you it didn't work! We have a bunch of untrained people trying to teach our young people! And that's only one illustration. I could give you more—community programs, the annual financial canvass, and others. We don't have a sense of continuity. We just change, it seems, because we want something new, not because it's good for us."

A congregation continues to be effective when it builds on its history. Having a feeling of stability means relying on a group of basic programs. They are year-after-year staples which are the yeast of the congregation. It is not appropriate in the church, or any organization, continually to change everything. All groups need the feeling of security that basic programs give. These tend to be worship, music, education, and missions. While everything changes over time, the degree of change should not endanger the basic solidarity of a congregation.

Given the discouragement which results from the two kinds of planning cited, some people might question the wisdom of planning at all. However, deciding not to plan is worse than either of the extremes resulting from planning. Without an annual planning session, people aren't exposed to new ideas nor do they have a chance to gain perspectives on the present. The danger of "doing it like we did last year" is very great.

A way out of this dilemma is to encourage enthusiasm while testing new ways against the present mode of functioning. For example, it would have been a better strategy for the congregation to keep its training program for church school volunteers and add the take-home tapes as an enhancement. The tapes would be an "add-on" rather than replacement of a needed program. Such an approach would have given some people, especially inexperienced teachers, further opportunities to learn at their own speed at home while keeping the tradition of a church-school-wide training event in which all the volunteers were together. The main provision of the strategy would be that both procedures be evaluated thoroughly during the year to see which produced better training results in that congregation.

The same approach of incorporating a new aspect into the existing program can be used by the congregation that never seems to get new ideas implemented. For example, finding two or three church school teachers to use follow-up absentee cards could give church school leaders information at the end of the year about the time used in keeping records and sending the cards, the number of people who came as a result of receiving cards, and the increased money spent on postage and church school supplies. With these data in hand, the planning session members can decide more intelligently how much further the idea can be pushed in subsequent years.

Developing a workable plan for a congregation depends upon compromise. The familiar way of doing business is comfortable. New ideas are exciting. Wedding these ideas requires careful negotiation. The old is not less effective merely because it's been done that way before. The new is not better merely because it's new. The planning committee must make the necessary compromises, deciding what of the old is to be kept, modified, or replaced as a new plan is produced. An effective plan incorporates both the old and the new. A plan requires both enthusiasm and a realistic implementation procedure.

In certain instances innovations or introduction of new programs must be put off for a year or two. This may be because of a lack of resources, the emphasis of a congregation's program, a special need which must be met, or an unwillingness in the congregation to consider change. None of these postponements for implementing a particular innovation should be viewed with alarm. Instead, the planning committee should use the intervening time as an opportunity to develop further the idea and program. The single adult program mentioned earlier is an illustration of this technique.

A planning committee is obligated to examine carefully the existing programs before introducing innovations or new programs. Many existing programs which aren't doing well can be invigorated by recruiting another leader, by readjusting expectations, by giving additional support through the governing body, or by making it a priority with subsequent publicity.

Salvaging and updating existing programs conserve much energy that can be used to initiate programs which are really needed. For example, it is easier to add a weekly luncheon to an existing senior citizens' program than it is to try to start a new program for those who live alone. If the luncheon is restricted to a particular type of senior citizen, such as those who live alone, that is the group which will come. The congregation, in this way, uses an existing program base, trained leadership, and experienced program developers to expand a program. This is working with the old program rather than trying to initiate something new.

It is the privilege as well as the responsibility of the planning group to try to find the means for strengthening current programs as well as to identify new program possibilities. When the committee does this well, the congregation has made its first step toward long-term change. The merging of the new and the old will have begun. The enthusiasm of the planning session will be retained even as the current needs and future possibilities become realistic targets for growth.

None of this will be accomplished without pain and conflict. Change requires both. However, a congregation grows as a result of pain and conflict. People can become key actors in the future they are creating. The process for pulling together the plan and the reality of its implementation is straightforward. However, it must be used with patience, concern, and integrity. It must enhance a congregation's programs, not replace them.

2

Fundamentals of Long-Term Change

Long-term change is a slow process. It takes time! Lasting change comes about because of skillful negotiation, determination, and the ability of a congregation to focus on its long-range purposes and goals while it lives in today's reality. Change comes as people will it and work together at it. A pastor alone cannot effect lasting long-term change. First it takes a planning group and then the entire congregation working in conjunction with the pastor to make change lasting.

Several fundamentals of long-term change are the focus of this chapter. They must be observed or change will not occur. "Listen" to the following conversation between the pastor and the treasurer.

"You know, if we had the money to buy a little computer and a copy machine, we'd be able to save several thousand dollars in printing and administrative expenses in a few years. We could probably pay for both of them with the savings."

The treasurer was silent for a minute before he replied, "You're probably right, Pastor, but I just don't see how we can shake loose the money to get started."

"Can't we take it from the capital improvement funds? A computer is a capital improvement rather than a current expense."

"That's true. The money would be invested in machines. But we can't touch the money in the capital improvement fund for at least five years. The board voted to keep adding to the fund because we will have to put a new roof on the sanctuary within five years." The treasurer shook his head. "We just can't do it."

"I know the board's action. It just doesn't make sense. We could really improve our office operation and free some volunteer time. The volunteers would be able to do more program work instead of using all their energy taking care of administrative details. The machines could help cut down on the detail time. You know what I mean?"

"Yes, I know what you mean. Machines like that can free time for some people. And you're right, a computer could make it possible to do a few things we can't do right now. I see how we could be more up-to-the-minute on changes in our membership lists, for example. We could probably get our mailings out faster if we did our copying here. And maybe we could even keep my financial records on the computer. You're right. The investment could pay for itself in a short time."

The pastor's enthusiasm increased. "That's right! And some of the volunteers who work in the office could do something else, such as use the phone to keep in touch with the shut-ins and make appointments for me to go see the visitors. They could help set up our calling program."

"Before you get too excited, Pastor, I have to say we can't do it. We just don't have the money."

"That's terrible! With the opportunities for increasing our efficiency, it seems like a sin not to be able to get started."

"I agree with that, Pastor, but we have to face reality. We just can't afford it."

The pastor sighed. He was frustrated once again. The treasurer rose to leave. He felt bad because it seemed that all he could do was oppose the pastor. It wasn't his choice to do that but he had a job, just as the pastor had his job. Both were looking out for the best interests of the congregation.

The pastor and the treasurer are both correct. The way in which the records of the church are kept can be revolutionized by a small computer. At the same time most congregations feel that money isn't available for an investment in machines. They would rather recruit volunteers to do work by hand. It seems the church insists on being behind the times. While the world has embraced technologies which free people to be more productive, congregations insist on labor-intensive activities which overburden their corps of volunteers. This is apparent in the conversation between the pastor and the treasurer. They know what should be done. They also see some opportunities for increasing the ministry of the congregation by using some money which could possibly be made available. But they are stopped by the problem of how to come up with the purchase price since existing money is earmarked for a particular project and can't be used.

Some pastors, confronted with such a problem, would forget about purchasing the machines. They would agree with the age-old dictum that getting by without spending money is the most important strategy for a congregation. They would concentrate on finding more people to work as volunteers.

Other pastors would see the lack of money for a specific project as a temporary issue that must be resolved. They would find some individuals in the congregation who would be willing to make a special contribution toward the purchase of the machines. Such people are known as the "pastor's angels" because they often give money for projects which he or she deems important to the congregation.

A few pastors would take the dilemma to the governing board of the church. These pastors would try to convince the board members to use enough of the money in the roof fund to purchase the machines. These pastors would also hope that people would replace the money used for the machines before the roof needed fixing.

Another strategy, one involving fundamentals of long-term change, is our concern. Pastors willing to follow this course would do the following things:

1. They would compute the cost of the machines, including the annual service and operating expenses.

2. They would figure out how this amount could be offset by more efficient use of volunteers, the reduction of outside printing costs, and expansion of program and ministry.

3. They would compile a feasibility study which would include (a) a method for accumulating money through special offerings, memorial gifts, a trust fund, and other means, and (b) set a target date for purchasing the machines.

4. Then they would design a strategy to involve the entire congregation in contributing to the project.

5. Finally they would help the members feel ownership and accomplishment when the purchase is made and the machines begin to be used.

Money Everywhere

This illustration of purchasing equipment outlines a strategy for those wanting to make long-term change. Let's use another part of church life to illustrate the principles further.

Pooling money from several accounts can make it feasible for congregations to participate in money market funds or special savings programs which earn interest on a daily basis. The simple act of pooling money from several accounts can be beneficial to all the accounts because they earn interest on a prorated basis for each group. Separately, most of the accounts are too small to qualify for such savings programs.

It takes money to make money. It also takes planning and careful budgeting to find money to begin saving. That's where many congregations are stopped. They think they don't have enough money to get started saving. A congregation intent on long-term change won't make that assumption. It will find money that is available by surveying accounts held in the name of the church.

Most congregations have money in several accounts: youth group accounts, church school classes accounts, women's groups accounts, building funds, mission projects accounts, and the church's current expense account. None of these accounts, for most congregations, has very much in it for most of the year. Yet combined the funds can be relatively significant.

There are two facts about money in the church: (1) money can be found for special projects which are seen to be useful; and (2) money is available in most congregations although there may be restrictions on its use. Given these two facts, a congregation must decide if it wants to change the process it uses for handling money. Money is important only as it is used wisely to further the ministry and outreach of the church.

Pooling money can be an important strategy of long-term change. It gives organizations an opportunity to work together with others in the congregation for mutual benefits. It requires discipline and accountability which are good things for treasurers in church groups. Investment of pooled money makes money which can be used for extras, such as additional contributions to a mission or for capital repairs. The benefits are substantial but in many congregations there is much resistance to the idea.

Resistance tends to focus on control of money and its use. Each group wants to be assured that no one is going to use any of its funds and that when money is needed, it will be available.

Given these benefits and resistances, what will it take to pool the various accounts so they can be invested? The most important thing is a decision by the planning committee that this is in the best interests of the congregation and of each of the organizations that will contribute money to the one account. This decision can be made only after research into the feasibility of establishing such an account and a presentation of facts and figures about the results of such a change to the planning group. The research should be done by a subcommittee of the planning committee or by the board if it acts as a planning group.

Once a planning committee decision is made, the congregation must be convinced that the project is worthwhile. A congregational presentation should include the following: (1) provision for adequate bookkeeping procedures; (2) a guarantee that the money of each group will be available as it needs it; (3) a provision for each group to keep account of its own money which it has contributed to the pooled account; (4) regular times for deposit and withdrawal from the pooled account; and (5) regular audits of the books of the pooled account. These are requirements of accountability and procedure which must be spelled out in an agreement form which is then negotiated with each of the groups.

The same process the pastor could use to purchase the computer is employed to move the above project from idea to actuality. This involved collecting data, developing a strategy for convincing the board, and setting a target date for purchasing equipment. The pastor relied on the facts collected and analyzed by a group of which he or she was a part; presentation of this data to the planning committee, the board, and the congregation; and setting a time when the equipment would be in place and could be used by the congregation. The pastor appealed to interest and logic. This same process can be used by a pastor and planning committee interested in initiating pooled investment funds.

The process for long-term change as illustrated above requires five steps.

Step One: Collecting data. Data for pooling money should include interest rates paid by various institutions, the minimum dollar deposit requirements of each money market fund, the availability of government insurance backing for each of the funds, withdrawal requirements, and the reliability of the fund's sponsor.

Step Two: Figuring out the most feasible ways in which the church can become involved in such a fund. This includes determining what moneys might be available, how much money needs to be retained by each treasurer, and the frequency and number of checks which may be written on each account.

Step Three: Discussing the issue. In the case of pooling money, this includes conversations with each organization and its treasurer. The discussions would focus on how the interest generated by the pooled fund might assist in program development and the safeguards and requirements for each group participating in the account.

Step Four: Setting a time for implementing the program. This might be a year or more after the idea is initially acted on by the planning committee.

Step Five: Conducting a periodic review and evaluation. The project must continue to meet the purpose and goals for which it was established.

These are the basic steps which need to be followed to accomplish long-term change. They involve building on the present while realistically working out a new future. To be effective, the process must change the attitude of a congregation about itself. This means it will have a new sense of self-identity which is lay oriented.

Staff or Volunteers

Creating a new attitude requires long-term change both in the thinking of the pastor and the congregation. This is clearly demonstrated in the issue of the use of volunteers in programming.

"We're large enough that we should think about having a part-time assistant. He or she could help with the youth, do some visiting, and preach once in a while."

"Do you really think we need somebody? We don't have that many active members."

"We have enough and we have quite a turnover. It's all I can do to keep up with administration and visiting our people in the hospitals. I don't have enough time to work very hard on youth programs and I'm behind on regular visitation. It certainly would help if we could have someone else do at least part of the new-member visitation."

"Why couldn't we train some volunteers to help with visiting? They could do as well as a part-timer."

"Maybe. But I'm not convinced about that."

Some pastors believe that adding staff members will automatically increase programs and membership. It is logical from their point of view that staff, who are paid to do a job, will be more likely than volunteers to do their assignment. These pastors overlook the fact that volunteers are vitally interested in their congregation and take on a job because it means something to them. With proper training, a volunteer is a valuable asset to any congregation.

What do you think the motive was behind the pastor's request? There may have been several; one could have been a genuine concern that work important to the congregation wasn't being done. Another motive, equally important, is one of status. The larger the staff of a congregation, the more it appears to be growing and successful. Yet another motive may have been the pastor's feeling that he or she wasn't competent to handle young people's programming.

The easy way out for a congregation looking to increase programming is for the appropriate committee to report that the pastor is overloaded and needs help. The congregation immediately sets about to find enough money to hire someone to help with the ministering. An unwary planning committee will easily succumb to the temptation to agree with the pastor. It will believe that a staff person needs to be added to accomplish the projected program. Unfortunately this avenue stifles program development as much as it helps to get it moving.

Assume that a congregation is faced with the issues presented by this pastor: the youth program is hurting and regular visitation isn't on schedule. What is the best strategy? If the history of the congregation is to ignore the pastor, it will do nothing.

If the history has been to do exactly what the pastor has requested, a search will be made for an assistant, probably part-time, who can do the jobs the pastor feels are essential. If the congregation is interested in working at a realistic future and is aware of the limits of budget, it will create an attitude among its members of "let's get it done by ourselves." Too long have pastors and congregations felt that strong programs require more staff members to administer them. In fact, not enough time or effort has been given to recruiting and training lay persons to do tasks which need to be done in the church.

At issue in many congregations is the feeling, among pastors especially, that lay persons have too narrow a vision of what the church can and should be doing. Since this is the case, it is up to the pastor to enlarge that vision. A pastor can enlarge the vision of his or her congregation through preaching, teaching, training, and informal conversations.

While enlarging the vision is helpful in creating new attitudes, the best way to change ideas and attitudes is to enlarge people's experience. This is done by giving them opportunities to grow in jobs which ask them to minister to others. Rather than complain about a lack of vision, the pastor, if he or she is interested in long-term change, will help a congregation revise its self-identity and attitude about its mission and who is in charge of accomplishing that mission. This is difficult. But it can be done in six steps. However, the key is not so much the steps but a willingness to take the time needed to train and support people who are developing new ideas and attitudes.

Step One. Remind the congregation of its purposes and goals. Purposes and goals are written down somewhere. If they aren't, this gives the planning committee or board a chance to interview the leaders of the congregation to find out their hopes and dreams. These can be used as the basic purposes and goals of the congregation.

Step Two. Identify the jobs being done by volunteers. List the programs dependent upon those jobs.

Step Three. List the jobs done by the pastor in the name of the congregation.

Step Four. Ask the board to help separate, from the two lists developed in steps two and three, the tasks only a pastor can perform. This will leave another list of activities which can be led by volunteers.

Step Five. Request the planning committee to identify programs that it is proposing which could be initiated and run by volunteers with the proper training.

Step Six. Develop a training program with the aid of the planning committee and the board, which will equip volunteers to do the tasks necessary to expand the program according to planning committee projections.

Choosing volunteers rather than paid staff makes program expansion possible within the budget of any congregation. The cost is time rather than a direct outlay of money. The pastor, board, and planning committee can work together to make certain that a recruitment program is set up, new programs are planned, and leaders are trained.

This strategy of depending on lay volunteers is healthier for a congregation than a strategy which relies on spending money for more staff to develop programs. The disadvantage of the process is that it changes a congregation's perception of how it functions and its attitude toward its mission. Some people, however, including this author, believe that such a change is the major attraction to the process.

Investing in Equipment

Recall the conversation between the pastor and the treasurer about purchasing new office machines. The treasurer saw a computer as a means for increasing the efficiency of his own functions. He evidently believed that with a computer the financial records of the congregation could be maintained better, more accurately, and in less time than could be done at present. He felt that the proper machines were a cost effective investment for a congregation. If a computer is an investment in efficiency, isn't it better to find the money to buy it now than wait another year or two?

The answer to such a question, regardless of the type of equipment being considered, is not easy to find. For example, one congregation decided that introducing labor-saving equipment might cause the two or three volunteers who worked in the office to feel they were no longer needed. It would make no difference that they could perform other services. Their perception was that a machine meant they weren't appreciated or wanted. Not only that, the volunteers' time of work and socializing at the church each week was being cut out. The personal interaction was very important to them.

Another congregation considering the purchase of new office equipment decided to replace its mimeographs and typewriters with a computer which could do word processing, a printer attached to the computer, and a copy machine. It was decided to do all the printing in the church office. The rationale behind this decision was the congregation's belief that it was enlarging opportunities for volunteers as well as making certain that the work of the office would be done on a time schedule over which the pastor had more control. The board felt that its purchases were consistent with improved efficiency and its goal of providing volunteer tasks for people who had new skills and wanted to work for the church.

Balancing people's feelings with the need for congregational efficiency is a continuing issue when attempting to be realistic in planning. It is at this point of balance that lay persons can be most helpful. Lay persons are especially sensitive about the feelings of others. They are more often aware of the negative impact of church decisions than are pastors. Therefore, it is the duty of lay persons to relay their perceptions to the pastor and the planning committee or board.

While the purchase of equipment is an investment in dependability, because time schedules and quality of work are more likely to be under the control of the congregation, the more important consideration is the impact of such an investment on people. A long-range view of congregational life attempts to weigh the immediate need and the long-term possibility.

This doesn't mean that one or two persons ought to hold up the modernization of an office or financial record keeping. It means that careful consideration and consultation with people is a necessity before major change is instituted. Such consultation may be done best by a lay person rather than by the pastor. Long-term friendships exist between lay persons and need to be retained as they continue to work together in the church. It is more likely that lay persons will be able to discuss the pros and cons of investing in dependability through equipment than would be a pastor, one of whose main goals is to assist the congregation's office to function efficiently.

Flex-Staff

"One of the necessities in a church that uses a lot of volunteers is a coordinator. You need one person to keep track of people and jobs."

"I agree with that. I've held that job in our church for the past year and let me tell you, it's hard work. Keeping the schedule and doing some training is all I have time for."

"That's my feeling, too. One of my big problems is trying to cover a person's job when he or she gets sick or something comes up and he or she can't make it."

"We put a work schedule in the office and then ask people who can't meet the schedule to find their own substitutes."

"How does that work? I've tried several things but not that."

"It works fairly well. Of course there are some people who don't know until the last minute and a few won't hold up their end of any bargain. But most people are considerate."

This conversation was between two lay persons from two congregations of about 350 members each. They were each called the "director of volunteers." Their churches couldn't afford new staff members and began using volunteers extensively. They became committed to using a large number of volunteers for program leadership and found it worked very well.

These two women had come into their jobs because their pastors found that they needed one person just to handle the volunteers. The women, both of whom had worked as volunteers for several years, had the right combination of skills, interests, and time. They were put in charge of the volunteer programs of their churches. They were responsible to see that all the volunteer work got done.

These congregations were employing the concept of flex-staff. Flex-staff is a combination of paid and volunteer persons who are assigned to jobs and who can be called when needed. In each of these congregations one person was in charge of scheduling and assigning volunteers to jobs that needed to be done. The only paid staff members in their congregations were the pastor and the custodian. Their organist/choir directors were part-time and, while paid, were not considered staff members.

Both of these women felt that a coordinator of volunteers was an essential for congregations with even a small number of volunteers. They had come to understand that just because someone volunteers to do something, there is no assurance that the work will be done well and on time. Someone has to make sure people know what to do, when to do it, and how to do it if any program is to be accomplished.

That's the reason the pastor in the earlier illustration wanted more staff. He felt that having an additional staff member would assure more control over the work and time of the volunteers. The two lay persons in the example show that it is possible for volunteers to do the work of paid staff if they have someone to whom they can turn for help when they run into schedule problems or become exhausted and have no more energy.

A budget doesn't have to include money for everything that is going to happen in a congregation. There are many activities which are free to the church but which are paid for by the time and energy of volunteers. It is up to the people who plan the budget, however, to include costs for supplies which will ensure the continued effectiveness of a volunteer corps in the church.

Assume a congregation decides to use several volunteers in place of paid staff. It is certain that these people will be part-timers. They cannot nor should they be expected to be full-time workers for the church. If there are several of these individuals, who is going to keep track of their coming and going? To whom do they turn when they need supplies? Whom do they call when they can't make it to the church at their assigned time? Who finds substitutes? Who maintains quality control? How do decisions get made about asking someone to take a different job because that person can't handle the job he or she volunteered to do?

The answers to these questions need to be found by the planning committee as it proposes the concept of a volunteer church staff. The pastor has more duties than she or he can perform and, in any case, shouldn't be a full-time personnel director. It therefore becomes the responsibility of the planning committee to find someone to be a director of volunteers. This someone must be sensitive to people and yet meet the goals and purposes of the congregation through volunteer work.

Such an individual will play a significant role in the long-term change process of a congregation. The reason is that the coordinator of volunteers is in charge of putting into practice the ideas of the planning committee.

The coordinator works with the pastor and others to recruit and train people who will lead programs. The coordinator finds and retrains the people who use the equipment that has been purchased to improve efficiency. The coordinator makes the planning committee look brilliant in its decision not to hire more staff.

Some pastors may protest that too much power is being concentrated in the hands of one individual. Not true. Persuasion is the only power one has when dealing with volunteers. Attempting to influence a volunteer's behavior is a frustrating task in many cases. Being a coordinator of volunteers is not a power-packed job for anyone. The position of coordinator of volunteers is vital but it is not a threat to the pastor, especially if the pastor works closely with the individual.

Long-term change comes about on a careful timetable of personal achievements which are welded together as organizational change. No one person is responsible for creating all the situations or activities which help others change attitudes and habits. It takes a lot of people working together.

That's the reason churches have governing bodies, planning groups, pastors, and coordinators of volunteers. It takes all of these groups and people working together at particular goals and for specific purposes before any change, short- or long-term can be accomplished.

The coordinator of volunteers is an individual working with the planning committee, pastor, and board to achieve new levels of program by building a flex-staff. It is realistic to have such a position but only when the task is clearly spelled out and accountability firmly established.

Goals and Purposes

"What I don't want is change for change's sake. I've seen too many changes that have caused a lot of disruption but haven't done a thing constructive in the long run."

"I agree with that but we can't live as if nothing is happening around us. We have to acknowledge that the world isn't the same today as it was five years ago. We need to keep up."

"I'm not so sure the church has to keep up with anything. After all, the message of the church is the same today as it has been for centuries."

"Now you're being difficult. We're not talking about the message. We're talking about reaching people, letting them know what the message is. We have to be modern to get them to listen."

"I know what you're saying. I just don't want the church to pick up on every fad that comes around. We are entrusted with a message that changes lives and we shouldn't dilute that by looking like some huckster."

"Gotcha! We have to keep our goals and purposes up front no matter what program we start."

These lay persons in a planning committee meeting were trying to sort out their direction. Their conversation about being modern was their way of focusing on what they were about as a congregation. They wanted to fulfill the commission of Christ, to go into all the world, and to make people disciples.

Long-term change is appropriate in the church only when it fulfills the specific goals and purposes of a congregation. This makes it critical for congregations to engage in long-term as opposed to short-term planning. It is not enough to look at how a budget is to be raised to keep a church going for another year. That is hardly following the purpose of the Christian church. The church was founded to accomplish the message of Christ in every age. The long-term purpose is establishing a community of the faithful in every age.

This long-term purpose gives to each congregation a challenge and an opportunity. The challenge is to find the methods appropriate to each situation to engage people in activities which help them become loving, forgiving, and serving in the name of Christ. The opportunity is to reach out into the community to touch other people with the message of Christ.

The goals of a congregation must support these purposes. While the goals may change from year to year, their primary function is to accomplish the purposes of the church. Every activity of a congregation ought to be tied directly to a specific goal and all the goals must be grounded in the purpose. It is the obligation of the planning committee to make certain the activities it proposes are in keeping with the purposes of the congregation.

3

Transition Time

Well, Pastor. You've really stirred things up. You've got us thinking about change, our attitudes, and how we might need to consider a new image. But that's all in the future. What do we do in the meantime? How are we going to get the money we need now so we'll have a future?"

The pastor looked at the treasurer and thought to himself, "I thought it was clear that what we do now will make the future possible. What's wrong with Jim? Can't he make the transition?" After another minute of silence, the pastor spoke.

"I guess getting people to think is the first step, Jim. What do we do next? We start with the future."

"But the future is out there somewhere. We live now. What are we going to do now?"

"The future isn't out there. We're building it with every decision we make today. Remember our conversation about fixed and discretionary budget items? We make a decision and pay for it from that moment on. Like I said, Jim. The present is where we start."

"You're a smooth talker, Pastor. But what I want to know is how we finance this operation in the present and in the future."

"Let's consider the next few months a transition time, Jim. We're going to have to work on four things as I see it. In the first place, we have to change the "make-do" mentality of the membership; then we will work on keeping the present in long-term perspective; next we will have to create a method for

41

making our fixed costs more productive; and, finally, we will set up the steps to get from here to there. It won't be easy, but that's what we have to do."

"That's a tall order. Where do we start?"

It looks as if the pastor and the treasurer are on the same team for a change. Unity among the leadership of a congregation is one of the critical factors in long-term change the pastor didn't mention. He was assuming it, which is a dangerous attitude.

When some leaders continue to hold out for another way of doing program, the split in leadership ranks is not helpful. The leaders in a congregation have to feel that they are working together in mapping out the future. Disagreements and conflict are inevitable during planning and strategy sessions but conflict is a necessary part of change. This makes negotiation and com-promise essential. A congregation can move into an effective future only when the leaders work together to make the new programs a reality.

Leaders acting as a team are important as the budget and the plan are merged into a realistic program. Each member of the leadership group must be committed and willing to work on the plans and programs which have been accepted by the board. A congregation does not function only through the pastor. It is active and effective because there are many people willing to work hard to make programs attractive and useful to members and community residents.

The spirit of cooperation and working together must be cre-ated and sustained. Just because an individual did not get her or his idea accepted, does not mean the individual has been rejected. It means that another idea seemed more practical and usable at that time. Leaders must learn this if they are going to continue to make insightful proposals which can guide the church. If they are convinced of the value of a proposal, they will make it again later.

Leaders must also be ready to deal constructively with those who continue to try to upset a decision. Every congregation contains people who are unwilling to make compromises and take risks. These are individuals whose makeup requires a risk-free environment. They do not want to change anything in the church because it has become their solid rock of security. Their attitudes and inclinations should be respected but the congregation should not be governed by their fears. A congregation must make a decision and follow that decision behind a group of leaders who are working together in building their church's future.

Getting behind a plan and working for its implementation does not mean this particular plan should be accepted continually as the ultimate answer for the outreach and program of a congregation. Every program should be evaluated and changes in direction must be made occasionally. The decisions to make these changes and to evaluate are best made by a group of leaders who are moving in the same direction.

Dissent and disagreement with the direction of a program should be taken seriously. Neither should cause panic but the leadership should listen to those who are raising questions. Again, this is done better by a group of leaders who are moving in the same direction. It may seem unlikely that a group which is committed to a particular direction would be more likely to hear dissent and take it seriously than a congregation with a pro and a negative contingent. Yet, this is the case. A group of leaders united around a core of programs has a wider interest range than a group, some of whose egos and personalities are tied to supporting a particular set of ideas, and some of whose egos and personalities are tied into opposing that same set of ideas. The pro or negative group can become a rallying point for killing programs and congregations. No congregation can continue for long when it nurtures dissent among its leaders and members.

Cooperation and compromise are essential when a group is involved in leadership. Each leader may be strong and be an active advocate of a particular aspect of program, such as the church school, worship, choir, and so forth. Yet the total leadership can agree on the *total* program and move in concert. This isn't lockstep by any stretch of the imagination. Dissent and disagreement are heard and evaluated. However, the program is effective because the leaders are working together rather than at cross-purposes.

The need for a unified leadership, pastor and lay persons, cannot be overstressed. The leaders must be willing, however, to be flexible in their efforts to implement programs and they must be willing to give people ample opportunity to adjust to the newness of programs being proposed. A vote on a program is only the first step, not the last, in its implementation. However, it is the vote from which the implementation can proceed.

One of the difficulties leaders face immediately after their decisions about the future program is dealing with the "make-do" mentality which infects many congregations. A fuller explanation of this problem is in order.

Making Do

I grew up in a small town in Illinois during a time of shortages. We kept looking forward to better times but in the meantime we had to make do with what we had. One man in our town seemed to thrive because of that philosophy. He could fix almost any mechanical device from cars to tractors to hay bailers to lawnmowers. He was a miracle man of sorts.

As time moved on and people had more money to buy new things, they began to ignore this man's ability. In fact, as people often do when they no longer need something, they began to ridicule his genius. When someone would persist in fixing up a tool or motor the epithet for that person was "Roscoe."

Roscoe was a man of transition. He was able to fix things because he was willing to tinker with them and to risk doing some things others would not try. He fixed rubber boots rather than buy new ones, for example. We have kits for that now, but back then fixing rubber boots was not done. Roscoe was the man of the hour, between the Depression and the great economic boom following World War II.

We have a little of Roscoe's temperament in our congregations, especially among treasurers and pastors who are over forty. They have lived long enough to know that there is a difference between need and desire. A need is something a person or congregation can't do without. A desire is something a person or congregation would like to have but doesn't need. Many treasurers feel it is their duty to act as the transition person, a conserver of the past as they wait for the future.

Every congregation needs a person of transition. As a friend suggests, "Every organization has to have an in-house historian. That's the person who remembers who and when. It saves a lot of time and lost motion because this person can recall successes and failures and give the reasons. Such a person is invaluable."

A transition takes place whenever change is in the offing. The time between making the plan and implementing the program marks the transition from the past to the future. It is a period of adjustment in thinking and in acting. It is a time when new thought patterns are being put in place and old habits are being challenged. It is a delicate time because how it is handled will determine whether or not the programs are ever implemented as well as the effectiveness of the new programs.

A transition time can focus on the past or it can be the bridge to the future. Roscoe's skills came from the past so that when we needed help with new gadgets, he couldn't fix them. He was great at old technologies and devising new schemes for using the old technologies. But he was tied to the past. He became a discard along with the Victrola and the old stand-up radio. He couldn't help us into the future.

In the dialogues between pastor and treasurer, we have seen the treasurer stressing the need for a transition process. This may make him sound like a worrisome person but the congregation can't do without him. He must be heard; a congregation moving from a past into the future must have a good transition plan. The one thing they don't need is the "make-do" mentality.

A make-do mentality is a set of compromises which delays change. For example, the congregation that decided not to purchase machines for the office but to recruit more lay persons instead was negating a forward push. Its feeling was that it was better to "make do" with the present system than to find a way to help the congregation move from a labor-intensive administrative use of volunteers to a programmatic use of them. Yet that congregation felt it was making the correct decision because it saved its money. It did not see that "making do" was a major limitation to program development.

Making do is the kind of thinking which thwarts the future and wrecks the plans of many congregations. They believe it is more essential to save money, conserve resources, or protect their heritage than it is to make significant changes in their programs. While it is important to do these things, it is more critical to look to the future than to the past.

During transition time hopes are stressed more than heritage. Transition is not a time for making do, but a time of creating new opportunities.

How does one deal with a transition time when the emphasis is upon making do? One way is to ignore and isolate those who advocate making do. This can be accomplished by taking them off committees and refuting their claims in emotional caricatures whenever they propose a make-do solution to a problem. Their critique of a proposed single adult program can be refuted by citing several single adults in the congregation who desperately need the church but because the church has no program for them, they are being lost forever. While this may be true, there are rational ways of illustrating the issue rather than dramatizing it.

Another way to deal with make-doers is to make them out to be the "bad guys." They are the ones who are never for anything but are always opposing new ideas. Citing them as culprits for the church not moving ahead is an effective method for labeling people and can accomplish two things: (1) make these persons ineffective as leaders; and (2) give them good reason to leave the church.

A third way to deal with make-doers is to do what they suggest. This usually ensures programs of the past and keeps the church mired in its tradition. Since the leaders, governed by make-doers, are more comfortable with the past, they may be more willing to work as program volunteers. But don't count on it.

A preferred method is to listen to the make-doers, take those suggestions which make sense, and translate them into positive bridges to the future. For example, a congregation decided it was time to hire a paid custodian rather than use a volunteer. The church's program was becoming more extensive and the building needed more attention than a volunteer could give. The maker-doer suggested keeping the volunteer on until it was certain that the congregation could afford the weekly fee for paid custodial work.

This suggestion seemed like a method for keeping things as they were with little prospect of change. The board felt manipulated by the suggestion and sought an alternative solution. The compromise, during a transition time, was to recruit two persons per week for six months to test the feasibility of continuing the volunteer procedure. After that time, if the work proved to be too much for volunteers, the congregation was committed to hiring a custodian.

While this process did not eliminate conflict, it provided a way to recognize the faithfulness of the previous volunteer, to suggest that more work was needed than could be done on a volunteer basis, and to point the congregation to a new way of thinking about custodial practices. This compromise provided for a transition time period which could be used constructively to change old habits and develop new expectations.

It is essential during the transition period to protect and reward people's work and integrity. At the same time, the congregation must decide to move in a different direction. This will require change. Since people are creatures of habit, they need time to rethink their ways of handling the congregation's functions. When a congregation is dealing with a make-do mentality, it must not negate people or their ideas. However, the congregation must choose options which serve as bridges from the past into the future. There is no need to feel that make-doers are obsolete. Their concerns are generally well intentioned even if a bit in the past.

It is important during any change to keep people involved. This requires skill in compromise and negotiation. Making decisions while keeping make-doers active but not determiners of program direction is difficult. Very important to the long-range future of the church and its programs is the willingness to encourage people to continue to make suggestions. When people feel that they've been heard, they feel that they're an important part of a congregation. When everything they do is negated, they feel frustrated and unwanted. This is especially true for make-doers during transition time.

The make-doers will be a troublesome group until their concerns are treated as suggestions which require negotiation. Then legitimate alternatives can be developed, many times with the assistance of the make-doers. They have to be part of the future, so encourage them to help build the bridges into the future.

Keeping the Present in Perspective

"You don't want me to spend so much time thinking about how we used to do things but, Pastor, all you can think about is the future. You're as guilty as I am in not paying enough attention to the present."

"You may be right. I have been so intent on keeping us focused on the future that I haven't kept the present in perspective. And we both know that what we do today will have a great bearing on our options for the future."

"You don't need to convince me. What I want to know is how to keep the past, present, and future in balance. We live now, so that's where we put most of our energy."

"True. But we mortgage our future by our attitudes and expenditures now. We can't have much of a future if we don't make the present a part of it."

"How about the past? What effect do you think it has on what we're doing now?"

"We're paying off the past. Our church debt was compiled before we came, the building was built, the way in which money was collected and spent—all were clearly defined by past attitudes. Everything we did then has a bearing on the present."

This philosophical discussion between pastor and treasurer is important. The present is the fulcrum or balance point between the past and the future. It is continually moving through time. We live in the present but each second becomes the past. The decisions we make now are historical when we relate them to someone else. However, the decisions and our talking about them affect future actions.

Keeping the present in perspective means that a congregation has to be continually alert to the opportunities it creates as well as to the obligations it assumes by the decisions it makes daily. These decisions are not for today only. Therefore, they must be consistent with the congregation's long-term goals and purposes. The church planning committee session of today will be history tomorrow but the deliberations and decisions will shape the next year, the next two years or the next twenty years of a congregation's life.

An earlier discussion in chapter 1 regarding fixed and discretionary expenses pointed out the need to keep the present in perspective. The focus in that discussion was on decisions about money. A differing aspect of keeping the present in perspective deals with the way in which programs are designed and implemented. Programs can lock a congregation into a pattern as surely as can long-term financial obligations.

The tendency of a planning committee or board which is considering the introduction of new programs is to pay too much attention to the wrong kind of future. Their future is full of "ifs" over most of which a congregation has no control. Some of these ifs concern the kinds of persons who move into the community. This is an issue which may be predicted but seldom very accurately. It does affect the church but a change in type of community residents allows enough time for a congregation to change direction slowly and consistently.

Another if is the economic situation. The general as well as specific economics of an area are often based on decisions which are made in financial centers many miles away from most congregations. Dealing with economics is a continual issue. The past is as good a guide as is available in how a congregation can best deal with most economic situations in an area.

For example, a congregation in an urban neighborhood was looking for a feasible future. It discovered that most of the members had moved to the suburbs. The majority of persons in the community were now Spanish-speaking. The congregation also determined that its income would suffer because a major employer in the community was closing its plant and moving elsewhere. Neither condition was under the control of the congregation. It could have bemoaned its bad luck and taken a wait-and-see attitude. Instead, members of the congregation decided, given their talents and inclination as a congregation and the needs in their area, that they would become an adult education center. The members would teach coping skills to new residents and help them become adjusted to their new environment.

A congregation should be concerned with those issues and events over which it has some control or which it can influence. These include such things as the kind of training it provides for church school teachers, selection procedures for leaders, tenure limitations on jobs, the kinds of worship services it provides, the visitation program, and the other services and programs it sponsors. These determine the future of the congregation's life and can be controlled and influenced by its decisions.

While it is good to have a resident historian, a person who

has in her or his experience or knowledge the major decisions and events of the past, it is equally important to have a futurist. This is the person who says, "How do you know we can't do it? If somebody else, another church, did it, so can we. We might not do it as well or have as many people, but if we want to get it done, we can do it." This continuing push to move beyond the confines of the past and present is essential for any congregation which wants to move from a plan into a realistic future.

It isn't difficult to keep the present in perspective, but it takes effort. The goals and purposes have to be remembered before decisions are made. This requires a plan which, in turn, necessitates a planning process. Neither the process nor the plan has to be elaborate. If a congregation functions primarily on verbal rather than written plans, the task of remembering may be more difficult but it is nonetheless possible.

The long-term purposes must influence current decisions. There is no way of building a future without a picture of that future guiding a congregation. The picture is an agreement of what the congregation's program is going to look like in three to five years. That picture will contain both the purposes and the goals which will ensure its becoming a reality. Keeping the present in perspective is done by continually comparing present decisions with the future picture so that what is done now will lead to what the congregation envisions for the future.

The treasurer's comments to the pastor about always thinking of the future are accurate if keeping the present in perspective is a concern. It is essential that continued reference be made to the future. The crisis with the roof today will influence how much money and effort can be spent on a program next year. Starting a program for drug or alcohol abusers next month will determine the image and program of the congregation for several years to come. Shutting down a youth program means three to five years of effort to get something worthwhile going again.

A congregation doesn't live only in the present; it lives with the images it created in the past. It also lives because of the purposes and goals it holds out for its future. When a group is so concerned with the past and the present that it cannot see the future, it is in deep trouble. It is in trouble because it doesn't have a guide toward which it can move. It is like a person who is cutting a lawn or sewing a large piece of fabric. One needs a point in the distance as a guide to cut or sew a straight line.

The point in the distance for a congregation is its plan, with goals and purposes. This is the corrective against which the present is tested. When this testing is done consistently, crises can be predicted and avoided, energy which would have been used for meeting the crises can be deflected to more creative uses, and the congregation can be more successful in fulfilling its hopes.

In order to keep in touch with the point in the future, however, someone has consciously to keep the congregation aware of it. In the conversations between the pastor and the treasurer cited so far in this book, the treasurer has been concerned with the present while the pastor has been pushing toward the future. The more appropriate way for such a situation to be handled is not to put two leaders into opposing forces but to create an awareness of the need for perspective among all the leaders. This can be done through training and practice.

Leaders who are trained to think of the present in the context of a future will be able to plan their programs and make their decisions in keeping with the goals and purposes of the congregation. Leaders without such training will have to be reminded about the goals and purposes at each of their decision-type meetings. In the long term, it is much more efficient and effective to train the leaders to keep the present in perspective than it is to have to remind them constantly.

It is always necessary for the planning committee and the board to keep in mind the purposes and goals toward which they are striving. Only in this way can the present be kept in proper perspective. The church will be able to live well in the present while moving forcefully into a future it is creating.

From Here to There

"You've done a lot of talking about transition, Pastor, but let's get down to specifics. How do we get from here to that future you're always talking about?"

The pastor smiled. "That's a problem, Jim. You and I have to work that out. You want to get started now?"

The pastor and the treasurer spent the next two hours working on the problem. In their meeting they listed the following steps which they would take to get from the present to the future.

1. Alert the church to the plan and its implications for programs. This may include a churchwide meeting to explain the planning process and the plans for the church during the next five years. The basis of the plans and the purposes and goals of the congregation should be carefully explained.

In addition to the meeting, articles discussing the plan and its implication for all programs of the church should be included in the newsletter for the next three months. The articles may be written by the leaders of programs for evangelism and outreach, missions, stewardship, youth, education, men, women, and the church school.

Announcements of the various elements of the plan should be made at the Sunday worship service. Some of the people who will be writing articles for the newsletter can be asked to condense their statements into two-minute talks. Two of them will speak on the last Sunday of each month for the following three months.

A member of the planning committee will meet with each of the organizations to explain the plan and its effect upon them.

2. Train the leaders who will be involved in implementing programs in the plan. This step can begin while the first step is in progress. The selection of leaders will be made at the normal election time for the congregation. Their training will include an emphasis upon the long-range goals and purposes of the congregation. They will be asked to relate their program intentions and expectations to the plan.

3. Make certain the projected resources are available. If the money is not available, the planning committee should find other means to support the plan. This might be through realigning finances, recruiting volunteers, or a combination of these and other strategies.

4. Set a date by which all the programs which are supported and for which leaders are trained will begin. These dates may be staggered so that everything doesn't start at once. Of course, some programs will be continuing rather than just beginning. The new leaders will be phased in as their programs begin.

5. Announce the beginning of the plan's program and celebrate it with an appropriate dedication at a worship service.

To an outsider, these steps are written in shorthand. They include a lot of work that goes on behind the scenes, work done by lay leaders and pastor alike. The important point, however, is that the schedule is clear, announced, and adhered to so that the plan actually becomes program.

The plan really began when the governing body affirmed it. From that point onward, it should be the guiding principle in programming. The lay leaders and the pastor should begin thinking and acting in concert with the major provisions of the plan. This means that they have to begin changing thought patterns, expectations, and actions to implement it. This shouldn't be viewed as a burden. After all, the people who thought up the plan are the church leaders.

The leaders' awareness of their obligation to move together toward the goals and purposes set by the plan will begin to change the thinking of the congregation. Note that the alerting step takes at least three months. This may be rushing the process a bit, but to spread it out longer is to invite disinterest and a sense of tiredness. A congregation can follow a carrot only so long before it begins to believe the carrot doesn't exist.

Leadership training may be a continuing program in most congregations. If so, the second step will be no problem. The focus may change so that the goals and purposes of the church are emphasized rather than the functioning of a particular group or program. The need to feel a part of the congregation's total program is important and should be conveyed to all leaders during their training period.

One of the most difficult issues will be making certain that the needed resources are available. A good bit of our attention has been given to this issue. It requires careful consideration of the facets of the plan, when to introduce which programs, how fixed costs may be used in a productive way, and how existing funds can be used best. This financial planning will be a concern not only of the finance committee but of the planning group and the governing body.

Resources mean people as well as money and facilities. A plan ought to specify how many volunteers are needed for each program to work effectively. This will allow the visitation committee and the pastor to recruit more effectively. The persons need to be recruited and trained before the programs begin but not more than three months before the beginning of the program. Most volunteers like to get busy right away. To train them more than three months in advance will take some of the edge off their enthusiasm.

Setting a date to begin a program is relatively easy. The fall is a good time for many programs to start. It seems like the natural rhythm of life for many congregations to start things in the fall. However, some congregations thrive during the summer and beginning a program in the spring would be more appropriate for them.

A few congregations do not have the same members all year. For example, a congregation in a resort community may have three dominant groups according to the time of the year: the home folks or year-round residents, the winter people, and the summer people. The congregation would begin the planned program for each group at the beginning of the season when that group would be most able to attend.

As each new program is begun, notice of its beginning should be made in the worship services of the congregation. A brief commitment service for the leaders would not be amiss. If several programs begin at the same time, one commitment service would be sufficient. If programs begin at various times during the year, the best effect would be to have the committal service for leaders close to the time of each program's initiation.

These five steps are not difficult to follow but they do require time and coordination. The plan must be workable and the programs must start on schedule. If the plan has been devised correctly, some programs will begin a year or two after the first ones start. In essence, a plan that's alive will always have a program in development stages.

Evaluation

Change happens because a group feels that an already existing program isn't working well or there is a gap in the program. Sometimes this is noticed when a new leader is appointed to a program and sometimes it occurs when people who are reached by the program speak of its inadequacies. Sometimes there is a formal evaluation; at other times evaluation is a hunch or feeling which is informally investigated.

Evaluation is an important element in developing a plan and implementing a realistic program. Every element of a plan ought to be examined closely by the leaders of each organization as well as by the congregation's governing body. The parts of the plan have to work together to meet the goals and purposes of the congregation and to address the needs of the members and those not now members who might be reached. The plan must be feasible, given the people and financial resources of the congregation. Determining all of this is evaluation.

Evaluation can be used as a wedge to move a congregation toward change. When it is used in this way it is an important strategic enterprise. Evaluation can also be used to point out the needs and opportunities to a congregation that has felt very good about its program. Indeed, every congregation ought to have this kind of evaluation occasionally.

What is often discovered in a thorough evaluation which is aimed at change is that a congregation has outgrown its goals and purposes. It has moved so far from them that new ones have to be established. When a congregation discovers this and draws up new goals and purposes, the subsequent program may be quite different from the previous one. Evaluation aimed at creating change gives church leaders a chance to develop new rationales and programs.

If this is the reason for evaluation, the cautions normally observed during long-range change must be observed. Go slowly, be careful in designing programs appropriate to the situation, get as many people as possible involved, and move ahead toward the new goals.

Evaluation is just as important when a plan is being implemented. Every plan is a part of long-term change and every plan needs to be evaluated each step of the way. For example, if resources for a part of a program cannot be found, the obvious evaluation of the membership is that the program is not important enough for its money and time. On the other hand, if a program is destined for closeout and people still clamor for it, this is an evaluation of a need. Evaluation is an essential part of every plan.

Changing direction, reaching out, and designing training programs are functions a congregation undertakes after it has evaluated its program. Without a continuous evaluation process, a congregation is in danger of setting up a plan, pronouncing it good, implementing programs, and failing to attract people. Nothing works entirely as it was planned. Through evaluation, the congregation discovers what was missing and what still needs to be done to make the plan more effective. Used in this way, evaluation helps a congregation to fulfill its mission.

4

Contingency Plans

Jim! We had a disaster this morning. The water heater broke and flooded the basement. We shut everything down but the plumber said it's going to cost at least $300 to put in a new one."

"That's not good news. Add that $300 to the $600 we have to spend for the roof and our reserves are nearly gone. I don't think we'll have enough money for the advertising or postage for that new youth program we planned for January."

"Not so fast, Jim. We're low now but we ought not count out the youth program because of the water heater. We'll just have to find some other ways of getting the word out so that we can afford the postage and advertising."

"That's fine with me but I don't know how we're going to do that. What do you have in mind?"

"Nothing yet but I'll think of something by Sunday. Listen for the announcements. If I come up with an idea, you'll hear it then. By the way, do you have any ideas?"

"Nope. But I'll listen real close on Sunday."

The next Sunday morning during the announcements in the worship service, the pastor made this announcement. "We have been planning to initiate a youth program in January, as you know. We had earmarked $200 for advertising and postage to send announcements to young people who have been associated with the congregation, as well as to those who aren't now active in any church. Unfortunately, this past week our water heater broke and it will cost over $300 to replace. Our other reserves must be used to fix the roof over the church school rooms. This means we have to adjust our method of paying for the new youth program.

"I talked with Jim, our treasurer, the other day and he said we have to raise the money; there's none lying around not being used. This morning, therefore, I am inviting you to do one of three things to help make our youth program a reality.

"One. You can contribute a few dollars toward the three newspaper ads we plan to use. These ads cost forty dollars each and will run once each week for three weeks.

"Two. You can contribute a few dollars toward postage costs. We plan to send one letter and a follow-up reminder to about one hundred and fifty youth. The total for that will be sixty dollars.

"Three. You may contribute some money toward the cost of the new water heater. The dollars given to that will make available money which then can be used for the youth program.

"Please make your contributions during the collection, but use the small envelopes in the pews or mark your check so that the treasurer will know your intentions. Thank you for helping make our youth program a reality."

Following the service the treasurer spoke to the pastor. "I liked the way you handled that appeal. I haven't totaled the amounts but I saw several small envelopes and at least one check which indicated it was for the youth program. That check was nearly enough to cover the mailing costs!"

"That makes me feel really good. You know, maybe the water heater breakdown was a blessing in disguise."

The treasurer laughed. "I don't think a flooded basement is a blessing at all. On the other hand, people knew about the youth program and what it is supposed to accomplish. Besides, you spelled out alternatives which told exactly what the money was to be used for. From where I sat, it seemed natural to give a little extra. There are always a few dollars that we spend that could be better spent. Today you told us how to do it."

Even the best-made plans can be disrupted by natural and human disasters. Planning committees ought to anticipate that all of their expectations will not be fulfilled as planned. That's the reason for contingency plans or alternative solutions.

It is neither possible nor necessary to create alternative plans for every conceivable difficulty. That would be setting up a plan with built-in defeat. It is much better to outline, during the planning process, some general alternatives for reaching the same goal. If this isn't possible, it is important to have a small group of leaders who can work together to find a solution to the unexpected problems that will surely arise.

In the water heater situation, the pastor met with two persons who were in charge of the new youth program. This small committee discussed several possible solutions including pushing back the starting time for three months. It concluded that the most desirable alternative was to ask the congregation for financial help. The committee members didn't want to set a precedent for every other new program but they were convinced that since the congregation had endorsed the plan and was enthusiastic about it, asking for support would not be out of place.

The response of the people at the worship service justified this decision. It was not an easy decision to make but it was acceptable and the response was positive. That's the major test of any decision.

A contingency is an unexpected event. A contingency plan is one in which some possible difficulties have been considered and solutions or alternatives to the plan have been discussed. A contingency plan is not put into operation or fully developed unless and until a contingency occurs. In many instances there will be no unexpected problem and to spend a lot of time developing a detailed contingency plan will be a waste of time. In such cases the original plan will suffice.

However, if an unexpected problem should arise, it is good to be able to turn to a small group, as the pastor did, and have them help work out a solution. Such a small group will be members of the planning committee and will be partially responsible for the anticipated program. They will be empowered by the planning committee to work out details of an alternative plan if an emergency should arise. In this case the water heater was the emergency, and the subcommittee met and worked out a procedure for ensuring the financial resources to undergird the program.

A planning committee or a governing body should appoint a

committee which develops contingency plans in case of emergencies. It shouldn't be necessary for the whole committee or board to meet to find a solution for a problem. A problem such as that of finding funding for the advertising for a youth program should be handled by a subcommittee.

So long as it doesn't change the plan drastically (if the subcommittee had decided the program should be put off for three months, the planning committee or board would have had to meet to concur with that recommendation or come up with a different solution), the subcommittee ought to have the authority to act on alternatives. In this case no new budget was being sought nor was the timetable being changed. The alternative was a method for raising a special budget item. If it hadn't been successful, the full committee would have had to meet to work out another solution.

A planning committee ought to consider possible difficulties before it introduces a plan for congregational approval. It is the committee's obligation to think of some of the contingencies which could occur. Alternatives, although not spelled out in detail, would then become a part of the plan. If the alternatives are not presented to the congregation, the church should be told that alternatives are being held in reserve to handle unexpected problems. This is an assurance of thorough planning.

Problems as Blessings

The treasurer was not convinced that a ruptured water heater was a blessing, but look what it did for the youth program: (1) it made people more aware of the priority the board was placing on this program since the pastor presented an alternative means of funding; and (2) it forced the subcommittee to devise another way of raising a small amount of money for advertising and postage. In this sense, the flooded basement was a blessing.

Emergencies or unforeseen problems are blessings if they call out creative solutions from a congregation. The emergency or problem becomes a burden only when the congregation allows it to be. Once again, it is the way in which a congregation looks at its life and mission that determines whether problems can be blessings.

Any plan is based on the premise that change is possible and some changes, specifically those which are included in the plan, will be positive for the congregation. It is reasonable to expect, therefore, that problems can be handled as puzzles which, when solved, will move the plan forward and facilitate change.

A few people believe that anything that occurs not covered by the plan will create a disaster. Not so. It is the attitude of a congregation that decides whether or not a happening is a real disaster. Even a physical emergency such as a fire, a tornado, a flood, or a windstorm can be a blessing (provided no one is injured).

The story of one congregation is illustrative. This congregation is in a midwestern city. One wintry day a few years ago the gas furnace exploded, causing a great deal of damage to the building. The congregation's leaders met several times to set up and review alternatives which seemed feasible. These included rebuilding, moving, or taking advantage of the situation to do some redesigning that they had wanted to do before rebuilding became a necessity. The eventual decision was to follow the third alternative, rebuild, but redesign so that the building would be more usable.

The congregation faced one major obstacle, money. The insurance would cover only half of what the members wanted done. They needed nearly two million dollars more if they were to do what they envisioned.

The rebuilding plan was presented to the congregation in terms of the mission of the church. The rebuilding was to be done to accomplish a particular purpose. The congregation was invited to participate by bringing to the altar, on a specific Sunday morning, the required amount in cash. On that day the congregation brought and laid on the altar the necessary two million dollars. The people were convinced that their building was important to achieving their purpose and fulfilling their mission.

Although the congregation had only about fifteen hundred members, they met an unexpected problem with a new sense of conviction about their ministry and backed that conviction with stewardship. They were able to meet an unexpected problem with creativity and resolve.

Some readers may say that this was an unusual situation and that the congregation was rich anyway. This isn't true. This church did have some persons who were able to give large gifts, but not enough to cover even a fourth of the needed amount. However, there was a strong desire among the members to make their building more functional so that they could better perform their ministry. It was this attitude which was the key, not the money or the disaster.

Quite a different type of resolve was displayed by the congregation whose pastor experienced divorce. The members loved both the minister and the spouse. They didn't want to take sides, but because of the emotions generated in the divorce, felt themselves being drawn into the controversy in a negative manner. The leaders met and decided the congregation must minister to both of these individuals.

The minister and the spouse were contacted by two different groups of leaders. In each instance the leaders expressed concern for both persons and indicated that the congregation wanted to support them. The leaders also made it clear that they were not siding with either of the two in their dispute although they wanted to help where they could. A settlement was finally reached. In the meantime, this congregation cared for, counseled, listened to, and helped work out financial settlements for both the pastor and his wife. They also found a place for the wife to live as well as a job and looked after the children.

This congregation, when confronted by an emergency over which it had no control, declared its mission and acted on it. The members met and developed a strategy as well as guidelines for their actions. They didn't solve the problems of the minister and the spouse, but they gave each of them and themselves as a congregation a new sense of what a loving community can do to heal wounds. This problem was a blessing to the congregation in that it helped it to act out its mission.

These three diverse problems in three congregations point out the need to develop a realistic contingency plan when confronted with an emergency. Contingency plans must be based on the following ingredients.

1. A basic plan must have been developed and presented to the congregation (which accepted it), along with dates for implementation. The plan of a congregation is its fundamental building block. Change ought to be based on the solid foundation of a purpose and goals which are contained in the plan. These are translated into programs which become the plan for

mission. A contingency plan can be set up without a basic plan, but it will be only a short-term emergency measure. To be effective, a contingency plan should be constructed on a plan which has been accepted as a blueprint for action by a congregation.

2. The contingency plan should be developed as an alternative strategy for achieving established goals. The contingency plan is not based on new goals or purposes. The emergency affects the way in which goals are to be accomplished, not the goals themselves.

3. The planning committee should select a subcommittee whose tasks include developing contingency plans. For example, in an adult education program in one congregation, the program is planned a year at a time with small groups being in charge of specific courses. If an emergency arises, such as the inability of a group to secure proper leaders, or if the selected leaders find they cannot come on the assigned dates, a subcommittee of the adult education committee deals with the problem. The subcommittee is composed of the chairperson of the group responsible for the program, the chairperson of the adult education committee, and the pastor. The program is expected to be carried out and these people are responsible for substituting leaders, adjusting the calendar by moving the affected courses to different months, initiating another course similar to the one scheduled but with different leadership, or canceling the course. The subcommittee decides what to do and then acts to implement its decision. The authority and responsibility for making these decisions have been given to these persons by the adult education committee. It has established the guidelines through experience and formal directives.

4. The contingency plan is evaluated by its results as well as by the planning committee and the congregation. No action in a congregation is accepted as if it were ordained by God. People make decisions and must be answerable to the bodies most affected by those decisions.

It is true that the three congregations cited here were able to treat emergencies as blessings. They were able to do so because they had or had created the mechanisms and had the will to make a disaster become a positive force for change. This suggests that most congregations can do the same if they prepare themselves to make every contingency an opportunity for fulfilling their goals and purposes.

This means that a congregation will feel that every emergency is a blessing in disguise. It will be able to move toward its goals with different strategies but with the same long-term effects.

Developing Reserves

"The reason we won this title is our bench strength. We had a better bench than they did. We beat them because we had better reserves than any other team."

Those words of explanation are from a basketball coach after his team had won a national championship tournament. He was pointing out the crucial role that reserves, in effect part-time players who aren't effective for long periods of playing time, have in sports. Reserves are spot players. They come into a game at a particular point to do a specific task. They are good and sometimes may play most of a game or even be starters for several games. But their greatest contribution is to come into a situation and be exceptional for a brief period.

Somehow or other the concept of part-time reserves, in this case volunteers, hasn't caught on very well in the church. Volunteers are generally treated as regulars. They are appointed to committees or assigned tasks which need to be done weekly or monthly. They are expected to be available to do their jobs without substitutions.

Most church leaders feel the recruitment of the "regulars" is hard enough. That's the reason most congregations haven't paid much attention to training "extra" persons or using people on a once-in-a-while schedule. The congregation has insisted on using volunteers on a full-time schedule and not changing personnel very frequently. The congregation doesn't feel it can have continuity in program if leaders keep changing. While this is at least partially true, co-chairpersons and other forms of shared leadership have worked well in many congregations. In effect, sharing leadership is calling on reserve volunteer leaders. Reserve volunteer leaders are called on as needed. They are willing and trained to do a job. The difference between them and regulars is that the reserves are treated as reserves. They are used on an as-needed schedule.

This means they must be trained and prepared for the tasks.

This is another reason congregations haven't been too eager to institute a reserve volunteer system. They are much more willing to spend time training those who they know will be used as volunteers.

In my book entitled *The Care and Feeding of Volunteers* I have discussed part-time volunteers and the need to allow people to be active for short periods of time. Setting up a group of reserve volunteers is a technique for the congregation that wants to be more effective in implementing its plans. Such a congregation will want to capitalize on the talents of all by using them as volunteers when they are available. This can be done only if the congregation is willing to use some people sparingly and others in an advisory capacity on occasion.

There is a small country congregation whose part-time pastor doesn't claim to be an expert in financial matters. When he has a problem with the finances, or lack of finances, in the congregation, he goes to a lay person whose tie to the congregation is through a relative. This lay person acts as a financial consultant to the pastor and the congregation. She is a reserve volunteer although neither the pastor nor the lay person consider her such. Yet her advice is free as is her time for the congregation.

A reserve volunteer may also be called upon for assistance by a congregation for a specific problem or issue. Such persons may be unable, due to time or inclination, to be active in the life of the congregation except to meet a special need. However, they are willing to give advice or may even take limited leadership for a certain time period. Many congregations use business leaders for special fund raising in building programs. These leaders are very active for a time but bow out quickly when the project is completed. This is the prototype reserve volunteer. Fortunately, reserve volunteers do not have to be business executives nor does a congregation have to wait for a building program to sign people up for short-term leadership. It is much more productive and sensible to have as part of the congregation's plan a process for building up its corps of reserve volunteers.

How does a congregation establish a reserve corps? It goes about this task in the same way it develops programs. The first step is to create a list of lay persons, their talents, and their interests. This has been done in many congregations as a part of the annual stewardship program. In other churches a brief survey form has been used. No matter how the list is accumulated, it should include all members.

The next step is finding out which of these people would like to be a part of the volunteer reserves. They should know that they may not be called on very frequently but they will be expected to attend a training session in their area of interest. They will also need to be contacted again at the end of the year to see if they are interested in remaining on the reserve list for another year.

The most effective use of reserves is to keep them involved. This means using them at least once or twice each year. A sports player cannot remain sharp if he or she never plays in a game. Competition keeps reflexes and skills in good order. The same applies to a reserve volunteer. This person must feel some involvement in the church. It is unlikely that an uninvolved person will make much of a contribution as a volunteer. He or she will not have the background or commitment of an individual who has been involved.

Reserve volunteers are lifesavers to a plan during an emergency. They have been trained, they are involved, and they can be called upon for short periods of time. Let's use the youth program as an example. Suppose the pastor's announcement hadn't produced the necessary money. The subcommittee could contact reserve volunteers who had been trained and who were willing to contact others by phone. Their job would be to inform members of the need and to give them the options outlined by the pastor at worship. They would not be selling the program or soliciting money; they would be doing what they said they would like to do, contact people to inform them about the church and its program.

If there are no reserve volunteers, when an emergency arises the regular volunteers must assume another job. They, by doing something they feel is necessary, are depriving other members of contributing time and energy to the congregation. In this sense, developing a corps of reserve volunteers is another means of helping all members to be stewards of their time.

People reserves are one thing, but congregations need money reserves as well. Many congregations exist on a day-to-day or Sunday-to-Sunday fiscal basis. They know their basic budget will be met but they just don't seem to have any extra funds for programs they would like to do. Once again the major culprit is attitude.

A congregation shouldn't have reserves if it intends to "live off" them. It should have reserves only to expand its mission. A congregation which can't finance its current program must review its commitment and style of operation. No congregation should live off the wealth of the past or store money away to assure its own longevity.

On the other hand, it is helpful to have some reserves available when emergencies arise. Reserves are possible when congregations change their attitudes toward what their mission is about. They will need to make long-term changes in the ways they think about money.

First, congregations must decide that money given to the church is for its mission. This mission is always undergoing change and adjustment. The money given is not to support a building or an institution because of its history. Money is given to mission which is always in the present and future.

Second, the congregation must be careful in its stewardship. If volunteers can do an adequate job, don't hire staff. If purchasing a new door saves energy, do it. If moving the worship service to an auditorium which is heated year round will save heating costs for the sanctuary, do it. If purchasing special machines allows a congregation more flexibility in its printing and record keeping, do it. In short, the church is entrusted with money and must use it intelligently.

Third, consolidate fund balances so as to take advantage of short-term savings. Every congregation has times of high income and low income. Use money market accounts as a place to help level out some of the extremes by getting interest on the high income periods.

Fourth, work as hard to develop money reserves as you work to develop any other program of the congregation. Since the money is to be used as mission, it ought to deserve as much attention and effort as education, worship, or any other activity of the congregation.

Reserves of any kind, money or people, must be used. They will do nothing for a congregation when they sit idly by. Developing reserves requires the planning committee to anticipate exactly how persons and money will be used to further the mission of the congregation.

Cut Back/Cut Out

"We can't ignore reality. We don't have the money. We can't continue to propose spending and programs when we can't afford them. We have to stop."

Silence. Then, in a tentative voice, a member of the governing board proposes a solution. "You've made it very clear that we have to limit spending. We need alternative ways of doing what we have planned. Perhaps we have to take some time or appoint a subcommittee to do some evaluation for us so that we know how important each item is. I don't like the word priority but it amounts to that."

Another member chimed in, "I agree. We have to decide whether we cut back on spending and programs or cut out some proposed programs. One deals with the present while the other is future oriented."

"That's one way to look at the situation, and probably the best from our perspective right now. But we have to remember that no matter what we decide, it will affect our future. Neither choice excludes the future."

"We know that, Pastor. Our concern is how we design that future. Should we strengthen what we have now without any changes? Or do we cut out some of our hoped-for programs and concentrate on one or two that will be very strong?"

It wasn't a very satisfying session but no meeting is easy or fulfilling when hard decisions affecting programs are being made.

Yet each congregation finds itself in these meetings at least annually. Plans are always greater than resources. When a congregation is faced with a decline of membership as well as a loss of income, decisions become that much more difficult. This congregation appeared to be going about the decision-making process in a logical manner. The governing body was dealing with the issue but requested more study.

Asking for a subcommittee to review plans and programs so that a decision can be made on funding seems like a good idea. However, the board should establish criteria such as: (1) we can't touch the youth program, it has to go on no matter what; (2) one area which might be possible to trim is the staff if we can design a good program for volunteer recruitment and train-ing; (3) our mission outreach may be increased if we hold some special events which educate as well as bring in some money; or (4) we must replace the heating unit this year.

These kinds of statements can give the subcommittee ideas about where to start their thinking. In effect the board, in setting up general criteria, thinks aloud and begins setting priorities. While priorities may have been established as part of the plan-ning procedure, time and experience tend to adjust them and new priorities must be set under pressure.

The subcommittee, in addition to having information about general priorities, must keep in mind the purposes of the con-gregation. These purposes will be another part of the priorities. Cutting back this year on a program which is the basis for expanded programs in the future will make it difficult if not impossible for the long-term plan to be implemented. For ex-ample, a congregation has decided to begin a single adult pro-gram in the coming year and expand it by adding an adult education program dealing with marriage and divorce the fol-lowing year. Because in this church's planning the single adult program is the basis for the adult education program, to cut it out is to cut out the possibility of the adult education component next year. This may be a consequence which the congregation cannot tolerate.

The subcommittee, to do its job well, ought to be aware of (1) the general thinking of the Board about priorities, and (2) the purposes and long-range goals of the congregation. These will serve as general guidelines. Accurate projections of income and realistic projections of volunteer participation in leadership for new as well as existing programs are also important ingre-dients for shaping the alternatives.

The subcommittee will be given a deadline by which it must report and the board will devote a session to consider its report. This indicates both to the subcommittee and to the board that the process will have a termination date and decisions will be made. Setting the date and work session forces the board to do more than simply delegate responsibility and thus postpone making the hard decisions.

When postponing occurs, the effort used to develop a plan is lost because the congregation drifts along on the decision of the treasurer and pastor who determine if enough money is available for each program. This means that the congregation has lost any say in its plan because, in effect, it has not chosen to be active in making hard decisions affecting money.

With the data outlined above, the subcommittee goes to work. It can be very specific and proceed down the list of programs for the congregation and make a recommendation for each. This tends to be the easiest form of report to develop and is one which the board can deal with most quickly. Everything is clear and the recommendations of the subcommittee tend to become the vote of the board.

The subcommittee can use an alternative approach which takes more time and involves the board in a more strenuous decision-making procedure. In this approach, the subcommittee, taking into account the purposes of the congregation, will deal with each program but will suggest several alternatives rather than make a direct recommendation.

One part of a report such as this would include a youth program.

Our purpose in youth programs is to involve each young person of high school age in on-site activities with others who are less fortunate, who have no interest in the church, and whose life-styles are different from the youth in our church.

The goals we have for the next year are: (1) a work camp at another congregation which needs volunteer labor that youth can perform; (2) a three-month evangelistic program for youth that would utilize different outside resource leaders; (3) a cooperative study program on life-styles, with another congregation in the community; and (4) a training event which would train at least a dozen new youth leaders.

We have looked at the budget for these goals, $3,000, and the ways in which the young people are supposed to help raise the money. The church's share is $1,500, which may not be available. We decided not to recommend on each item but are posing three alternatives.

1. If the board decides not to fund any of these goals, the young people may be able to find funds for part of the program. This will make them decide what is most important to them. It will also decrease the credibility of the board in the eyes of the youth.

2. If the board decides to give half of the money and designate it, the three parts of the program requiring most of the budget—a work camp, an evangelistic program, and training new youth leaders—would have to be considered separately. Any one of these

might be deleted but the long-range effects of deleting any one of them could seriously hurt the youth program.

3. If the board decides to fund all of these goals, this will reduce the church school budget by $1,500. This could result in a loss of teaching materials and supplies, a reduction in attendance at training sessions by the teachers, and a new limit on the audiovisual aids to be used in teaching and training.

None of these alternatives is easy but the probable results of choosing any one of them are clear. When the full report is available, the board can make decisions which are intelligent, although perhaps painful. This procedure of letting the board select from alternatives will increase discussion and focus the board's attention on its long-term goals and purposes.

Priorities Within Priorities

"What you people have brought back to us is another planning task. I'm not sure we want to go through that again. We asked you to tell us when to make our cutbacks and cutouts."

"You asked us to do more than we could. It's up to the board to set new priorities. If that means making priorities within priorities, that's what it's going to have to be."

"Priorities within priorities? What are you talking about?"

"It's not very complicated. You have agreed on a plan and have listed the most important goals. You have set a date by which each program is supposed to start. Now we have discovered that we have neither enough money nor can we get any more volunteers. So now we must look at the programs and decide how we can implement them and still remain within our budget. In my words, that's setting priorities within priorities."

"It may be just a play on words."

"No it isn't. We are proposing that the original plan be kept as the basic guide for our congregation. We couldn't find any reasons to throw it out and start again. We felt it was much smarter, therefore, to rethink the starting dates and maybe push back some programs or push forward the dates for discontinuing other programs. We are asking you to consider rethinking the development process."

Many times when a congregation is faced with the need to cut back on its spending plan, it gives up the original plan. Indeed, many congregations don't feel they can accurately project their resources, money, or people, so they don't even plan.

That's not good stewardship. A congregation has an obligation to plan and then to follow that plan. The persons holding the conversation here are trying to adjust to realities which were unexpected. These people are discouraged and may feel that they have wasted a lot of time putting together a great plan only to have it scuttled by lack of money.

The subcommittee felt differently. It said that the basic plan was good. What the board needed to do was to look inside each priority and redo the activities that make up each program. This is exactly what the subcommittee did with the youth program in the example cited previously. The board was not asked to cut out the youth program and substitute another program for it. Rather, the recommendation had to do with the four major activities which made up the full program (work camp, evangelistic emphasis, joint study, and leader training). The board was being asked to make priorities of these four elements so that the youth program could still be treated as a priority of the congregation.

Each program of a congregation has elements or pieces to it. In the church school, for example, the pieces may be teacher training, basic supplies, audiovisuals, student take-home papers, parent alerts, and the like. If the church school needs to cut back, it can do so by trimming all of these elements by a particular percent or it can determine that some elements are not necessary to effective teaching (such as parent alerts or student take-home papers). This is setting priorities within priorities.

In planning, the different elements of each program should be clearly defined. This takes more thought on the part of the planning committee but it makes the final plan much easier to deal with when emergencies arise or projections run afoul of reality. When programs are put together as components, it is much easier to make hard decisions about what to postpone, cut out, or cut back while still moving ahead toward the original goals.

Consider a denominational stewardship program. It consists of six or seven components, each of which can be limited if time, money, or volunteers aren't available. Dinners to explain the budget and program to the congregation may be eliminated and time made available in the worship services for this task.

Instead of sending four letters, two letters may be sent and announcements made in the regular weekly bulletin or news-letter. Instead of buying audiovisuals, a congregation may develop its own. The point is that stewardship programs are naturally divisible. It is up to a congregation to decide what it can afford and then to do the program as effectively as it can.

It will take a little practice, but planning groups can develop the technique of making certain that each program is divisible. It is better to do this at the early planning stage than to wait until an emergency has occurred and a subcommittee must be assigned the job of sorting out what is to be eliminated. As a result of this early planning, it is easier to make decisions quickly enough to respond to an immediate cutback in resources.

Immediate Decisions

It's nice to be able to call a committee together for counsel and then have its recommendation affirmed by the board. This procedure works most of the time if planning is a normal process of the church. However, there are times when someone has to make a decision on the spot. Who does that?

It depends. The immediate decision-maker is determined by the planning setup and authority process of a congregation. In the illustration regarding funding for the youth program, the pastor made the decision which necessitated a new procedure for raising money.

In another setting the person in charge of a program may decide on the need for an audiovisual presentation, attendance at a training session, or purchase of new equipment. These decisions will need to be affirmed by a board but such approval may be after the fact. The board may not meet until after a training session has been held, or the new equipment may be on sale for only a week. The immediate decision-maker is usually the pastor if he or she knows the fiscal situation of the congregation at the moment. However, very few pastors will make immediate decisions without checking with the treasurer or chairperson of an appropriate committee.

The important thing to remember about planning is that it anticipates many situations which could call for immediate decision making and provides a procedure for handling a potential crisis. In fact, planning is a method for cutting down on crisis management and promotes a new attitude of being ready for most situations. Those designing the plans must designate the person or persons who can make immediate decisions if an immediate need arises which has not been provided for in the plan.

5

Doing More with Less

It seems as if this congregation is always looking at a deficit. There must be a better way to handle our affairs than we're doing."

"I'm afraid there isn't, Jill. Money comes in but there are more things to spend it on than we ever imagined possible. When we get the boiler in good shape, the gutters and downspouts start leaking. When we think we have a good insurance plan for the pastor and secretary, the rates go up. When we increase our church school attendance, the cost of materials increases. There never is an end to the cycle."

"But we have to do something! We have less money today than we had last year at this time. And we're intent on enlarging our program. Could somebody tell me what we're going to do?"

This cry for help is not unique to the present age. It has been a common theme through history. The reality of life is that most people, and congregations, must learn to make do with less than they would like to have. It is an age-old problem of wanting to do much more but not having the resources. This is no cause for despair. After all, that's the reason for planning.

Planning enables congregations to be better stewards of their resources. It's not that congregations haven't been careful about their money. They have. Many have been frugal to the point of cutting out programming for no good reason. Stewardship creates a new mindset regarding the use of resources.

Being a steward of the congregation's resources is a concept relatively few finance or planning committees in congregations have accepted or understood. Yet a realistic planning strategy is based on congregations being stewards of their resources. What might this mean? Many church people think they are users of money rather than stewards of it.

Being a steward of money has surprising implications. Not only do stewards receive and account for money; they are supposed to make it work. Not only should the money work, but it has to work in such a way that it accomplishes the purposes of the person or group to whom the steward is accountable.

Most of us have heard of stewardship in relationship to the money-raising campaign which comes around once a year. Actually, stewardship and the every-member visitation program it encourages are a part of the planning and budgeting process in many congregations. Unfortunately, most people relate stewardship to taking pledges and raising money.

While most people may equate raising money with stewardship, that's only part of the story. Consider the principles of stewardship being used in relation to conserving energy. When the energy crisis affected congregations, they began to think in stewardship terms. They wanted to make the best use of their energy. Light switches sprouted little signs telling people to turn off the lights when they left a room. Thermostats were repaired, zone heating was used, parts of buildings were sealed off during the winter or summer, and insulation became an important expense.

These changes to conserve energy represent stewardship in a very practical sense. The cost of energy made it impossible for many congregations to have enough discretionary money for developing new programs; therefore, conservation and energy saving became important.

Another concept which is little understood is that of being a steward rather than a caretaker of the church's facilities. If a steward's task is to use facilities to accomplish the purposes and goals of the congregation, caretaking becomes only a minor part of the chores of trustees. Only a minor part of their job is to make certain that the roof doesn't leak, that the rooms are painted, that the furniture is safe and in good condition, and that the ventilation systems function properly. In addition, their job is to make certain that the activities allowed in the facilities further the mission and purpose of the congregation.

Stewardship deals with time and talents as well as with money. That's the reason some congregations include an interest finder in the every-member visitation packet. This little survey form is used to identify potential volunteers. The use of the interest finder raises the issue of being a steward of the congregation's volunteers. People dedicate time and energy to the church's work because they believe in what it is doing. When a congregation doesn't honor their efforts by failing to give them a job or by not allowing them to work for short periods or by not reassigning them when their talents don't fit a particular task, it is not being a steward of its volunteers.

These concepts of stewardship are explored in this chapter following a discussion of leadership, which is another form of stewardship. While many members feel they hired a pastor as a leader, this is not the way congregations function. A pastor must be a leader but he or she will be effective only when there are strong leaders among the laity. Strength begets strength. Shared leadership between pastor and laity is necessary if planning is to become reality.

A scarcity of resources is common. A leader who can illustrate what stewards can do is not common. Leaders and the attitude that it is stewards who will make long-range changes in its programs must both be created.

Having fewer resources to work with invites a congregation to use them more wisely and to make those resources work harder. A pie-in-the-sky attitude? Not at all. Resources are to be used, not collected and kept. There may be less money or fewer volunteers in a congregation in any given year but that is not the end of the world. A congregation with few members and little money can do mighty things if the members are inspired by faith and guided by principles of stewardship.

Leaders or Facilitators

A congregation can "do more with less" only after its purpose is clear and a plan to accomplish the purpose has been developed. The plan is essential. It is the blueprint for action. Implementing a plan, however, happens only through the work of a leader. In chapter 4 the pastor decided that a projected youth program was so important that he was willing to become a leader. He took the initiative by calling a committee together to discuss the new situation. Together they reviewed several alternatives before deciding on a plan of action. In the end the alternative chosen was bold and was implemented by the pastor. He had acted like a leader and the results were positive.

A facilitator works differently than does a leader. Given the same situation, the facilitator probably would not have done so well. He or she would not have taken the initiative to call the group together nor would the facilitator been the one to implement the plan of action. The facilitator would have helped the committee develop its plan and may even have come up with the idea used by the pastor. However, it is one thing to help a group come up with an idea and a feasible plan; it is quite another to challenge a congregation to face its plan and make it work.

The line between a leader and a facilitator is fine since the leader functions to facilitate in many situations. The difference between the two is more a perception of role, an attitude, than a matter of skills.

This isn't a criticism of facilitators. Groups need someone to prod, push, and keep them on track. Small group research has much to say about the positive role such a task-oriented individual plays in planning and decision making. A group needs a facilitator to help move it toward its objective and goals.

An effective facilitator doesn't allow a group to bounce from one topic to another. It is for this reason alone that a congregation needs a facilitator in its formal committee meetings. Issues need defining and the group must make decisions. A facilitator helps in these tasks.

A pressing need in many congregations is for leaders. A leader symbolizes the group spirit, internalizes its purposes, and continually challenges the group. The leader is not only task oriented, but also creates an emotional atmosphere within the group which ensures accomplishment. A leader's commitment rubs off on others.

However, a leader can't lead unless people want to follow. The leader can't inspire unless the congregation is convinced of its purpose. The leader can't help a church choose among alternatives until there is a plan. A leader is part of a group and tends to represent the best thinking of the group.

Thus, a leader is an essential part of a congregation's planning process. He or she helps make certain the congregation intends to follow its plan and helps develop the strategies which must be followed for the plan to be implemented. When necessary, the leader creates the enthusiasm and generates the energy the congregation needs to implement its programs. The leader helps the congregation stride creatively and confidently into the future. The leader keeps reality in the plan through personal discipline, effort, negotiation, charisma, and drive. These are the qualities which make a person a leader.

Leaders use whatever means are necessary to get a specific task done. The leader's tactics will be different according to the need at any given time. In one situation the leader may act as a mediator between two groups, each of which wants to tailor a plan so it benefits them more. In another setting the leader will be critical of the congregation because of its unwillingness to follow its purposes. At still another time the leader may be the inspirer and challenger to give the church the courage it needs to tackle difficult tasks.

The leader doesn't allow a congregation to rest easy because it has done something. A compliment will be given as deserved, but the church's work is never done. Witnessing is never completed. A leader will be aware of this and will help the members find new energies to push on to accomplish their goals.

The church is a witnessing community of believers. As witnesses to the power of Christ, the church community cannot be led by facilitators whose goal is to achieve consensus. Witnessing doesn't create consensus. It proclaims a message. This means the church needs leaders. The church, especially in times when it is necessary to do more with less, needs committed leadership.

Why be so adamant? Because the church has a message which it cannot contain. Its business is not to make people happy and feel good. It doesn't major in immediate gratification. Its purpose is to call people to the saving grace of Jesus Christ. Accomplishing that purpose requires discipline, sacrifice, and singleness of intent.

In order to keep a congregation on this track, the church needs leaders who can show people how to be witnesses. The task is never easy but it is a necessary one. In order to change, to put into effect any long-range plan, a congregation must be led to be witnesses rather than to be obsessed with a "how're we doing?" mentality.

The best way for a congregation to assure this attitude is to train its leaders to be leaders. The congregation must demand that anyone who is going to lead do just that. This means that the individuals who are chosen to be leaders must inspire, be aware of the environment in which the church functions, know the resources the church can raise and call upon, have an instinct of timing, and be willing to make hard decisions regardless of popular opinion. These kinds of leaders are required by congregations that sincerely want to put their plans into operation.

A lesson continually relearned by the church is that ministers must be leaders. In the past two decades the church has trained ministers to be facilitators. Society has helped enforce this emphasis by its focus on popular psychology which stresses immediate personal gratification. Many lay people have tolerated the facilitator-type clergy as they have watched and waited for the return of clergy leadership. They want to get behind a leader.

These lay persons have not waited in vain. There are signs that the traits of leadership may be reappearing among the clergy. For example, a few years ago one denominational leader declared that he could not function as a leader because people wouldn't let him. Recently in a public address he stated that he had to act like a leader no matter what people thought. The change was not in the people, it was in the denominational leader.

In the church the clergy's primary function is to lead. Yet clergy can be effective only when there are effective lay leaders. A leader can present a vision but there must be others who can challenge and correct that vision with visions of their own. Give and take, negotiation and revision, are elementary parts of planning. This takes leaders who keep the purposes and goals in perspective so that they can help the congregation make certain its plans are feasible and can be implemented.

Money

"What do you mean, be a steward of our money? We are careful how we spend it. Isn't that being a steward?"

"Yes, in a way it is. But a steward's responsibility is much more than being careful about spending. A steward in charge of money for a congregation is charged with managing those finances. We have to be careful how we spend money but we have to use money so that the congregation's goals and purposes are accomplished. That's a lot bigger job than just being careful about spending."

"A steward manages the money of a group to accomplish the group's purposes and goals? That's a new wrinkle. I always thought our job as a finance committee was to keep the church solvent. I never thought of us as stewards."

"That's for sure. When we get down to the red ink, we don't have to worry about being stewards. We have to find the money to pay the bills."

"Yes. And that's quite a trick in this congregation. Our people are mostly older and live on fixed incomes. We just haven't any leeway. I don't see that this talk about being stewards applies to us at all."

The finance committee of this small congregation was reacting negatively to the pastor's suggestion that it be a steward of the church's money. The committee didn't feel that it had anything of which to be a steward. Yet planning requires a shift in focus from treating money as something with which to pay the bills, to regarding it as a commodity which is used to achieve particular results.

Let's put the matter of money and stewards more dramatically. A congregation knows it will receive, through pledges and offerings, a certain amount each year. While there may be some fluctuation in this amount, these variations are usually very slight. In addition, the congregation knows when it will receive the bulk of its income. For example, the Easter and Christmas seasons are high income times while the summer can be a very lean time.

Stewards manage their financial resources to maximize the benefits of the high income times by investing and savings plans. By the same token, they will find the means to relieve the pressure on finances during the dry times. The latter may mean using lay persons as preachers during the pastor's vacation period, using lay persons to develop special educational curricula for periods of the year rather than purchasing all of the materials used, or using music groups from the congregation instead of paying for substitute musicians.

In addition, the congregation can do things to help level out the giving. This may mean introducing a pledging system which asks for regular weekly or monthly gifts. In other situations, being a steward of money will mean emphasizing an annual every-member visitation program. In other congregations the effort to level out the giving may include automatic check-off processes. (These are automatic deductions from a person's checking account and credits to the checking account of a congregation. This has been done mostly in the insurance and mortgage fields. However, in recent years banks have begun to offer this service to churches.)

Being a steward requires active involvement. A finance committee which functions as a steward of money helps people understand needs, becomes committed to the goals and purposes of the congregation, and keeps in communication with the members. A committee functioning as a caretaker of funds reacts to situations and is generally on the verge of a crisis.

Think about it another way. Suppose a congregation had to earn its money rather than depend on gifts. What could it offer its people to guarantee an income? Since the product of a church is an effective ministry to people through Christ, one would expect quality worship, music, education, counseling, and organizational activities which develop Christian community. If people paid a congregation in terms of what they receive, and its quality, how many churches would continue to exist?

While most people would not consider church programming in this light, it is one way a steward looks at a congregation's program. The church is supposed to provide its members with some services. These must be of an acceptable quality. The trouble in many congregations is that people have been so used to receiving second- or third-rate services that they would be shocked by an improvement. Being a steward of money requires a new attitude. Quality is important since the product changes lives. We are talking about being servants and proclaimers of Jesus Christ. This demands stewards who expect the best for their resources.

Stewards also make certain that the money of the congregation is used most effectively. For example, are the dollars spent on clergy paying for quality leadership? This might be answered negatively in many churches. Indeed, in most churches, questions can be raised about what tasks are to be done by a pastor and which can be done by part-time or occasional workers, some of whom are volunteers.

Too many pastors spend too much time being secretaries, mimeograph operators, and maintenance people. These are not the jobs a minister is trained to do even though he or she may enjoy doing them. A minister is an educator, counselor, worship leader, resident theologian, and administrator of a congregation. When these roles are not assumed by the minister, they usually aren't covered. When the roles are performed poorly, the members are deprived of quality services.

One part of a planning process must be to identify the tasks to be done by the minister and those which can be done by lay persons. It is then up to the congregation to make certain through its committees that this division of labor is observed and the work is done.

Another question for stewards of money is, "What have we been doing that doesn't need doing?" The answer to this question comes from the planning process and relates to ministries and activities which have run their course and need to be discontinued. One of the most difficult decisions for a congregation is deciding to discontinue something. There is always some mythical "they" who will be offended if a ministry is stopped.

In reality, few people want to support an activity which is not effective or helpful. Such activities can range from an after-school church school program, to youth music, to two services of worship, to too many staff members, to a community outreach program. The list can be extended but it is more important that it be customized by each congregation. Things have a life cycle and must die. The same is true for programs. The needs for programs change and programs must die so that others can be started.

One of the discoveries an evaluator makes is that people have public and private opinions about almost every program in a congregation. The public opinion generally supports the visible or elected leader's opinion. For example, a pastor's pet project might be to have an intergenerational church school class. Many people come because they are loyal to the pastor, not because they are excited about the class or its content. Their private opinion may be that the pastor can't teach very well and they would rather do something different with their time. But they come to the class anyway.

When an evaluator reports that a majority of the people in the class would rather it be discontinued and a different form of adult education be introduced, people can agree with this anonymous majority without seeming disloyal to the pastor. Stewards discover how they can improve the programs of the congregation and how the money can be managed better by doing research into people's private opinions about the church. Hard decisions are made with solid information. That's a basic tenet of planning and allows congregations to be better stewards of their money.

It takes a congregation with a strong sense of stewardship of its money to make the decision that "we've spent enough on that program and must discontinue it now because it no longer is a part of the purpose of our congregation." This is a hard decision because it tampers with the history and image of a congregation. That's the only way, however, for a congregation to be intentional about its life and its future. It must decide to stop some things as well as to begin others. Planning helps a congregation align its programs to its goals and purposes. Reality is making those plans become programs.

Being realistic in planning demands decisions which affect the lives and hopes of a congregation's members. These decisions are frightening to make and often are very unpopular. They are necessary, however, when a congregation begins to view itself as a steward of its money rather than as a caretaker of financial accounts. The concept of being a steward of money adds a new dimension. It creates the feeling that "our money must work hard so we can accomplish our goals and purposes."

Facilities

"We spent six weeks traveling through the United States looking at church buildings. It was a most fascinating experience."

"How do you mean? A church building is a church building. How different can you get?"

"Quite a bit different. We found some churches whose sanctuaries were merely large rooms. Others were like theaters in the round. A few were part of large office buildings. Some were not much more than modern chapels such as the kind you might see in an airport."

"I didn't know there was such variety. I thought church buildings were sort of stamped out of the same architectural mold. Oh, I know there are a few offbeat types but mostly they're the same. Now you tell me this! What is one thing you can say to sum up your observations?"

The man and woman sat for a minute and then she spoke up, "The thing I noticed more than anything else was that few of these buildings were designed to promote Christian community, to signify that a worshiping group of Christians were the owners of the buildings."

"That's right! Everything else seemed to be going on but there wasn't a permanent place for the community to worship together. In one church the pews were pushed back against the walls and the room was used for recreation after school, lunches for the elderly at noon, and a meeting place for community groups during the rest of the time."

"But that wasn't typical, was it? I mean, you only ran across a very few like that didn't you?"

"The number that were so extreme was small, that's true. But we found that church leaders were so interested in doing other things with their building that they seem to have forgotten that its primary use is for a worshiping congregation."

During much of our history Protestant churches were used as the gathering place for the community and often the place where community meetings were conducted. They were the focal places of social as well as religious activity. They were looked at as the solid foundation on which the community was built.

Much of this imagery was superficial but enough of it was true to give church leaders a feeling that their building was supposed to be more than a facility to house a congregation. This meant a compromise in the style of the facility so that community residents would not be distracted by religious symbolism when they were gathered to nonreligious functions. In short, many of the earlier facilities were multifunctional, with the telltale signs of religious worship movable so no one would be offended during public meetings.

Perhaps a multifunction facility is thought by some current religious leaders to be an ideal. It symbolizes the church as a center of the community, as a focal point for activities of a community nature. In one sense, such an ideal represents stewardship of facilities. The buildings are put to use and are beneficial to many worthy groups in the community.

However, a church building is not a community place. It is constructed to provide a place of worship for the gathered community of the committed. It is not multifunctional with removable religious symbolism. Instead it has a distinct purpose, which is to house the community of the committed as it learns, plans, worships, and acts. It is not to be a meeting place for a variety of groups except as each group furthers the purpose of and helps the congregation achieve its goals.

Being a steward of its facilities requires a congregation to make certain the buildings are used to further its purposes. This does not limit activities so much as it focuses them. Plays, musical performances, and various types of programs can be given in the sanctuary so long as they promote the purposes of the gathered worshiping fellowship. After all, the building was constructed by such a community so that it could worship and meet together to achieve its goals.

This means that any ceremony held in the facility ought to be directly related to the purposes of the congregation. For example, weddings and funerals for members of the congregation are an extension of the ministry of the worshiping community. By the same token, providing the church facility for a wedding merely because a couple likes the location and beauty of the sanctuary may not be a part of the congregation's ministry.

The educational part of the building has been constructed for the same purposes as the sanctuary, to enhance the fellowship and education of members. It is not, nor should it become, a free space for any worthy cause that might wander in. All parts of the church building are constructed for the purpose of being a place where Christian community is fostered and the goals of the congregation are fulfilled.

As a steward of its facilities, a congregation is obligated to ask of each activity, "Is this a legitimate outreach of our ministry?" When there is any doubt about the activity or question about the group, the answer must be no. The congregation is not in the business of giving a home base to all groups or activities which originate in the community.

On the other hand, some activities which are started in the community need to be housed in the church. A single adults program which might have begun in the community can find a home in the church if the program helps the congregation achieve its goal of outreach ministry.

A critical element of facility use is that the building gives support and legitimation to the activities held in it. There is no such thing as "the group only meets there, we don't support it." Allowing a group to meet in a facility is a form of support. That's the reason that being a steward of facilities means making those who use the building work hard at helping the congregation achieve its purposes.

Finally, being a steward of a facility means that any group which uses the building must help pay for it. The "free lunch" argument can be used with the church as with everything else. There are costs associated with any use of a building. Noncongregational groups using the building need to be assessed costs for keeping it open, maintained, and secure.

A building is an investment by a congregation in its future as a witnessing community. The building is an effort to symbolize to the community that this group is going to make a difference in the life of the area. Once constructed, the building must be used by the congregation to fulfill its goals so that its promises to God and to the community might be kept.

Making Costs Productive

Three areas of fixed costs are in most congregation's budgets: ministerial support, building (including maintenance), and outreach funds to and through the denomination. (If the congregation is a house church run entirely by volunteers, the budget may have other categories of fixed expenses.)

Recall that fixed expenses are those over which a congregation has little control. For example, if the costs of fuel oil, natural gas, and electricity rise dramatically, the congregation must pay them no matter what else gets paid. It has no control over these increases. If a minister is hired, it is important to pay a minimum salary and then to provide other benefits. The salary and benefits need to be raised each year if quality ministerial service is to be continued.

Fixed costs may appear to be a culprit which can wreck a

congregation's plans for the future. How in the world can a congregation save enough money to invest in new equipment if it has to increase its heating or cooling bill by 20 percent a year? That is a question which has echoed across this land for the past ten years. But it tends to evade the issue. The real question is, How interested in developing a new future is this congregation? If there is interest and commitment, there are techniques to do almost anything.

An obvious solution to the problem of fixed costs is to have some group help share such costs. For example, in several cities new ethnic congregations share buildings with existing congregations. These new congregations usually meet in the afternoon or early morning and give something toward the cost of operating the facilities. This allows them to begin without a lot of overhead, while assisting the existing congregation by contributing toward maintenance and building upkeep.

A requirement in any type of sharing is to be certain of the parameters. This is especially important when sharing ministerial time or allowing other groups to use church facilities. The parameters must include: (1) a time limit; (2) a specific use; (3) the amount of reimbursement; (4) the kind of reimbursement; (5) when reimbursement is due; (6) how adjustments in the agreement can be made; (7) who speaks for each of the partners to the agreement; (8) the time period in which the agreement is in force; and (9) an evaluaton process which can result in cancellation or continuation. Often the congregations are not prepared to enter into such an agreement because they have not figured out how sharing fits into their plans and purposes.

This suggests the need for serious discussion of sharing as one way to help a congregation meets its goals and purposes. The discussion will occur during the planning sessions and will also be a part of the board agenda when it considers the plans for next year and beyond. Since sharing will affect everything a congregation does, it must have widespread assent from the members or it can severely curtail both stewardship and evangelism.

Stewardship will be affected when a congregation enters into a sharing agreement to conserve resources rather than redirecting resources into new program endeavors. People, seeing the new income, will feel less obligation to support the church.

Evangelism will be affected because the feeling of many members will be that since more persons are using the building or the minister is meeting more people, evangelism will naturally occur. They will feel less need to be active in going out to reach people for the church.

The parameters, therefore, must be discussed and enforced; but, more important, the concept of sharing must be worked into the plans of the congregation. Sharing must be a means for assisting in programming and expanding the mission of the congregation or it loses its appeal for the long-term benefit of the church.

Let's look at the parameters more closely:

1. *A time limit.* This refers to the hours or days in which sharing is to occur. For example, the agreement might be for a group to use the church facilities on Tuesday evenings from 4 to 10 P.M. This would include the time needed to set up and clean up as well as the time for the meeting or function.

2. *A specific use.* The nature of the use must be clear in the agreement. If the use is a dinner meeting, this should be spelled out, as well as how many kitchen utensils, tables, table coverings, and the like will be needed. Spelling out the details will avoid controversy later.

3. *The amount of reimbursement.* This is critical. The issue is not to have another group shoulder all the costs but to share costs. The reimbursement ought to be reasonable yet be able to be negotiated upward or downward based on experience.

4. *The kind of reimbursement.* The form of payment may be services. For example, a group might use the church facilities and agree to do all the custodial work instead of paying cash. Or a congregation may share its minister with another congregation which shares its education director. If personnel are shared, it becomes very important to have a joint committee which is composed of persons from each of the sharing groups.

5. *When reimbursements are due.* An agreement for a specific use with a particular amount of reimbursement must include the time of payment. This must be adhered to as with any other contract. In fact, the agreement should contain a clause which sets a default period, such as thirty days beyond the due date, which can be enforced. Usually this kind of default means the agreement becomes void.

6. *How adjustments in the agreement can be made*. Experience usually points out areas where the agreement ought to be modified. Perhaps the estimate of time is too long or not long enough, or the amount of reimbursement is too much or too little, or the form of reimbursement doesn't work out. Any one of these conditions calls for adjustments and the agreement ought to tell how this can be accomplished. It usually takes the action of the governing body for each group, conveyed in writing, for changes to be made.

7. *Who speaks for each of the partners*. The official position of a group is given by its governing body. The person who signs the agreement does so as a representative of the group. This individual can discuss problems and issues in order to clarify the agreement but any changes of an official nature must come from the governing body itself.

8. *The time period when the agreement is in force*. This can be for a year or two or for a five-year period. The date of this time period should be specific, such as January 1 through December 31 in a given year.

9 . *An evaluation process which can result in continuation or cancellation*. This gives each group an option for the future. It doesn't lock either into an agreement which it might find constricting and not in keeping with its goals and purposes.

Sharing, given these parameters, can be an exciting and fulfilling way of cutting down the fixed costs. Again, the reason for sharing should not be survival but expansion of ministry. This procedure ought to be used only by those congregations that have a plan to include sharing as part of their ministry.

Another method for making fixed costs productive is to use the resources of those groups which are supported by fixed costs. For example, if money is sent to the denomination, a congregation ought to get as many services from denominational staff as is possible. This might include such things as teacher training, leadership seminars, materials, mission speakers, and visiting preachers. It is wise to use these resources as a means to expand and enhance programs. This method ought to be a part of the plan. A week of evangelism with a denominational staff person can be an exciting addition to the visitation evangelism program of any congregation. A stewardship program conducted by leaders trained by denominational staff can be very effective. Mission speakers for a month can be a useful way to focus on missionary giving. The point is that the resources are being partially paid for by the congregation so it ought to use them as a part of its planned program.

A third method for making fixed costs more productive is to change what they are paying for. For example, a minister's job description can be changed so that he or she becomes primarily a trainer of volunteers. The volunteers do most of the work except for most preaching, handling the sacraments, and performing weddings or funerals. The function of the church building can be changed from being available at all times to being primarily a meeting place for worship, with all the other meetings being held in private homes.

This method requires considerable effort to change habits and perceptions. People are used to having ministers perform most of the functions of a church and it will take effort to get them accustomed to any change in his or her job. It takes less effort to move the meetings into homes but the congregation will need to find hosts or hostesses who will serve with grace and skill on a regular basis. Some members might view holding meetings in their homes as a part of their mission through the congregation.

These three methods for making fixed costs more productive can be used in most congregations. Smaller congregations might find the sharing model and changing the function descriptions most helpful. Larger congregations might want to use models two and three. No matter which is chosen, the use of any of these alternatives makes fixed expenses pay for program expansion.

Volunteers

"We collected a lot of information from our members during last year's every-member visitation. What have we done with it?"

The chairman of the board looked at the pastor and said, "That's one you'll have to answer, Pastor. I don't know that we've done anything with it."

The pastor grinned. "We have data overload on our members. We know more than we need to and we haven't figured out the best way to use even a fraction of the information."

"You mean we went to the trouble of writing all that stuff down and it hasn't been used? What a waste."

"I'm afraid you're correct. It has been a waste and we're paying for the mistake. People have been calling since the visitation, asking when they would be used in a job. We've had more calls than you can believe."

"What I can't believe is that there wasn't a plan to use people before the data were collected. It sounds as if you didn't think anybody would volunteer."

"We didn't expect a quarter as many to want to do something for the church as have called. I thought we had a plan but evidently it wasn't enough."

It would be nice to report that this is an unusual situation. It isn't. Congregations have been pushed into the interest-finder solution to recruitment and have not been prepared for the response. It has been a disaster in many congregations and its use has created ill will and disillusionment among potential volunteers.

When they join a congregation, people agree to support it with their time, talents, and money. This three-point agreement is often ignored and the emphasis shifts to frequency of attendance and money support. A part of the reason for this realignment of oaths is the lack of a program for volunteers in most congregations. Too often only a few people are asked to become involved in the program of the congregation, except as spectators or attenders. They are seldom asked to give energy or time or to use their talents.

This is not a deliberate tactic of congregations or of their leaders. Wasting or ignoring talent and energy which could be used for the church happens because congregations don't know how to use their volunteers. They have no idea of what is involved in being a steward of volunteers.

Being a steward of volunteers has the same obligations as does being a steward of facilities and money. The efforts of volunteers must be utilized to help the congregation achieve its goals and purposes. In addition, however, volunteers must be able to achieve some of their own personal religious goals by working for the congregation. They must find community, love, appreciation, and fulfillment in their activities. If they can't, the congregation is not being a steward of its volunteers.

Being a steward of volunteers includes at least the following requirements:

1. Each volunteer must have a clear and concise definition of the job he or she is being asked to do. Job descriptions are written in some congregations but in most the nominating committee is keeper of the task descriptions. Ideally, a planning committee will create a list of needed jobs with suggested qualifications. The jobs, when done by volunteers, will fulfill the goals and purposes of the congregation.

2. Volunteers should be offered a choice of time commitments. If the job is teaching in the church school, it may be wise to offer a teacher the option of working one or two quarters rather than insisting upon a commitment for a full year. If the job is to assist with typing in the office, specific time slots, days, and months can be offered. Volunteers need to schedule their time the same as do those who work full time in the church.

3. Volunteers ought to be used when they are available. A woman who teaches literature in a public school system is asked once a year to give one month to teaching an adult class in her congregation. She sets the month and the topic is agreed upon mutually. She would not be able to give her talents or time if she couldn't help set the time or the topic.

Of course not every job can be negotiated this way. However, even typing can be negotiated if the congregation is willing to allow people to work in their homes. Some people want to come to the church to work because they like the fellowship of being with others. Other people just don't have the time to come to the office but can do a lot of work if it can be delivered and picked up from their homes.

4. Volunteers must be recognized for what they have done. This doesn't have to be a "big deal" but it is a necessity. A letter, phone call, or a card does the trick nicely for most people. Special recognition for long or meritorious service can be in the form of a certificate or an award.

5. Volunteers must be trained. Some congregations call sessions they use to acquaint volunteers with their jobs "training," while others call it "orientation." Regardless of what it's called, at least one session of training per year should be scheduled to orient and train new volunteers. This training should be conducted each year whether a couple of people, one person, or a

hundred or more persons are being trained. Training is a necessity, not an option.

The training will include a review of the goals and purposes of the congregation; an indication of how each job the volunteers are performing will help achieve the goals and purposes; financial support and reimbursement for each job; ongoing training opportunities available from the judicatory or ecumenical agency in the area; rules for use of the facilities; availability and ordering of supplies; and where to turn for help. In some congregations it will be necessary to describe the role of the coordinator of volunteers, how one submits a resignation, the process of evaluation used with volunteers, and the committee which receives reports about the volunteers.

People give a part of their lives to the church when they volunteer. It is the church's obligation to help them use their time and talents creatively in fulfilling the ministry of the congregation.

Being a steward of money, facilities, and volunteers may be a new idea for congregations. The concept of stewardship requires an understanding of the use of resources so as to achieve the goals and purposes of a congregation. The resources, including leaders, money, facilities, and volunteers, are precious parts of the congregation's life and must not be wasted or underused. Thinking as stewards helps a congregation to become sensitive to the needs and desires of its members as well as to get excited about its mission. A stewardship attitude can help the congregation make the resources work harder to achieve more, even if there are few people and little money.

6

Conflicting Priorities

Realism is being able to picture an ideal, put that ideal into a purpose, create goals which can attain the purpose, develop programs which implement the goals; and then being able to negotiate between the conflicting priorities of people and groups within the congregation in order to make the programs successful. A plan is a blueprint for action; it is not action. Implementing programs is action. Any time there is implementation of programs, conflicts occur.

Negotiating priorities is necessary at every step of the planning and strategy development process. Being able to negotiate while keeping the purposes and goals clearly in focus is a difficult but essential task for the congregation which is serious about making its plan work.

What do we mean by negotiate? In political parlance it means striking a compromise or working out a deal. It involves give and take among persons or groups who want to accomplish something they consider important. The critical part of negotiation is making certain that the compromises deal with the mechanics of implementing a program rather than with the program's substance. For example, the women's organization of a congregation wanted to hold a fair for four days in the fall. It was a tradition the women wanted to continue. In addition, the fair would make money to pay for some important outreach efforts. Unfortunately, this year the fair was scheduled during the same week that the senior citizens' group wanted to use the church for its fall "senior alert," a community-wide program of education about resources for senior citizens.

Both groups had authorized the dates and put them on their calendars before checking with any other church groups. When the conflict in dates was discovered by the pastor, a work session involving the leaders of the women's and the senior citizens' groups was scheduled.

The focus of their conversation was the date, not the validity of either program. In other words, they negotiated the mechanics of implementation, not program substance. The result of their deliberations was a compromise. The senior citizens' outreach program was to be advertised at the fair and put back one week. The feeling was that the additional advertisements at the fair would increase attendance at the senior citizens' event. In this instance, the negotiations worked well.

This illustration points out some of the reasons why negotiations are necessary even when a plan is in place. A common difficulty in a congregation is lack of communication. This can be between groups, between the pastor and leaders, or between leaders and members. The nub of the problem is that leaders of organizations often assume, once they have made a decision about a program, that everyone automatically knows about it. They also may assume that a brief notice in a bulletin or newsletter is sufficient to alert everyone on all other committees and in all groups.

It would be wonderful if that were the case. It isn't. People have a lot of things on their minds. They may see a notice but it may not click that something they're planning is in conflict. It is therefore important that someone within the congregation pay attention to calendaring and to getting the word out about programs time and time again.

Another thing the illustration points to is an important task of the pastor. He or she called the two groups together to work out a deal on the dates in conflict. The objective was to keep both programs, to give them strength, and to try to ensure their projected results, not to make one less important than the other.

This is management for results. The aim of this kind of management is not to jeopardize the church's programs, not to emphasize one group over another, but to try to help all groups in the church carry out their ministry. This requires skills at negotiating, but more important, it demands that the pastor keep the plan for the congregation in front of all the groups all the time.

A third point in the illustration is that the potential crisis was discovered far enough in advance so that it was solved before a crisis could occur. In fact, the negotiated result of the conflict was to blend the fair with support for an additional program of the congregation. Crisis prevention is as important as being able to solve a crisis. Most crises in the church can be avoided if someone is aware of the total program of the congregation and takes action to negotiate problems before they grow into crises.

The solution of the date problem substituted rational thought for emotional panic. Each side could have insisted that its program had highest priority. Both could have argued with great emotion to keep the date. But that didn't happen. A solution was worked out which strengthened both programs. This can happen only when the issues are worked at carefully and objectively. In certain instances this takes some doing, but it is the best way to proceed.

Finally, the illustration points out that a total church program is more important than any single part of it. When the programs mesh into a comprehensive plan, they can accomplish a purpose. When each organization continues to function as if its own programs were the most important, the congregation suffers. The congregation suffers because its program lacks wholeness.

These are the issues which are the focus of this chapter. The desire for making a plan operative means a lot of work for many people. How they go about that work, the spirit they have toward each other, the willingness they have to work together for the good of the congregation, and the effectiveness of the pastor in alerting and negotiating are all factors in achieving the goals of a congregation. One person or group can't make a congregation's plan work well. It takes the whole congregation to implement its plan.

Communication

"Who's in charge of advertising in this congregation?"

"No one. We have looked and looked but no one wants to take on this responsibility. It's important, but we just can't seem to find anyone."

"Well, then. Isn't it the responsibility of the secretary or you as pastor? You're the only ones who know everything that's going on. You should be responsible."

"If I did that job, something else would have to suffer. I'm not certain you would agree that I can cut back on any other task and I'm not willing to give up my study time since that's important to my sermon preparation."

"What are we going to do? We have to get the word out about our programs. Even if it's only to our members, we have to let people know what's going on."

This is a dilemma with no easy solution. The lay members of the governing body were aware of the need to communicate with the congregation as was the pastor. Unfortunately, they could not come up with a strategy to meet the need.

What is the basic need they're concerned about? It's to keep the members and constituents of the congregation aware of the needs and opportunities of the congregation as well as to invite them to become involved in the program. This type of communication traditionally has been done through announcements at worship services, bulletin notices, weekly or monthly newsletters, and telephone committees. Some congregations may use all of these but most churches are limited to one or two practical means of communication.

People respond best when they are asked directly. Word of mouth requests for time, energy, and money are the most effective way to recruit people, to get them involved, or to have them contribute. However, this is very time consuming for the leadership; in many cases it requires time which leaders simply do not have. That makes the use of a communication device which can reach most of the people regularly and inexpensively very important.

Announcements of programs, events, and needs at worship services are used in most congregations regardless of other forms of communication. The problems with this form of communication are: people may not hear accurately; every member who might be interested in a program may not be present at the service(s) when the announcement is made; and the brief time available for such an announcement limits its effectiveness.

A monthly or weekly newsletter that goes to members and constituents is another common form of communication for many congregations. While the content of the newsletters may be everything necessary to alert people to the total program of the congregation, the medium used may be flawed by neglect, sloppiness, or lack of experience in duplicating.

Congregations must keep in touch with their members but how can it be done better? What's the solution? There are several suggestions which can reduce conflict among priorities. Each of these suggestions ought to be incorporated into the plan. The planning committee ought to work out, in general terms, the type of communication and the time when it should go out. Subcommittees can work out details after the plan has been confirmed. Included in these details is the designation of the person or group responsible for getting the word out.

Setting up a communications procedure includes the following steps.

1. The general form of communications, i.e., bulletin, worship announcements, and newsletter are most often handled by the church office (volunteers, paid secretary, and pastor).

2. The calendar for all the activities of the congregation is kept in the office or on a bulletin board just outside the office (or in a central meeting place where members of the congregation can refer to it when they come to the church).

3. Each organization is responsible for checking dates and activities on this schedule before program dates are made final. This will help avoid conflicts in programming.

4. Each organization and group will designate a person (or persons) who will be responsible either for all the publicity of the group or for publicity for each program, or for a particular time such as a month, quarter, or half year. The person (or persons) will make certain that the program dates are put on the central calendar, that newspapers receive information about the programs, and that announcements are made at worship. Dividing the responsibility among several persons in the organization often works better than letting one person take care of all the publicity, especially if the congregation is depending on volunteers.

5. When the congregation and its organizations use several people to communicate with the members and the public, it is a good idea to give them communication guidelines. These may be simple rules about what goes in the announcements, who is

the person most likely to respond, how those reading or hearing may participate in the church's programs, when the event or activity is scheduled and where it will be held. Additional information needed will include deadlines for making sure materials are in the office for inclusion in the bulletin or newsletter, newspaper deadlines, and to whom the announcements are to be sent or given.

6. If several people are responsible for communication of programs during a year, it becomes the responsibility of the chairperson of each committee and organization to make certain that the communication work is being done properly and on time. This usually necessitates an annual meeting with the communicators so they know their responsibilities and are aware of the expectations of the group regarding getting the word out. At this meeting each of them should receive a copy of the guidelines along with deadline dates.

7. At this same meeting communicators will be assigned specific times when they will carry out their responsibilities and the names of all the other communicators. They will also be told how to go about making a change in their schedules if they have a problem with the time period assigned to them.

While these are suggestions about setting up a communication procedure, the more important consideration should be the message of what the congregation's programs are trying to do for people. Communication in the church seeks to get people excited about and involved in the congregation's programs. In this sense communication is interactive. Word goes out from the congregation but it is requesting word back. Communication is not public relations in the sense of trying to sell a product. It is public relations which informs for commitment.

Since the purpose of communicating is to let people know about opportunities and needs of the congregation, the content is as important as the method used. As with the other processes of realistic planning, communication must include the purposes and goals of the congregation. Attracting more members or a better offering might be good things, but only when in accomplishing these they are achieving the congregation's purposes and helping it meet its goals.

Implementing plans is not an easy or simple task. There are a host of "housekeeping" details which must be considered and cared for at this level. Communication is a housekeeping detail. It helps people get to events, lets them know where they can volunteer their energies, and informs them concerning the specifics of results. These kinds of details must be communicated if a congregation is going to expect its plan to be implemented.

Realism in planning takes care of such details. Setting the time for and identifying the person or group responsible for communication should be part of the planning process. Producing guidelines, meeting with communicators, and keeping abreast of their activities are responsibilities of church leaders. The planning process should spell this out in clear and precise form. If this is not done, the chance for conflict among priorities will increase.

Managing as Stewards

The management model used by most clergy and lay persons is the business one. Its emphasis is upon "hard-nosed decision making" and "the bottom line." These phrases sound like what the church needs but when they are put into practice in a congregation they are quickly acknowledged to be inappropriate. They are out of line because they are assuming success to be an increase in dollars, more members, and an abundance of programs and activity in the building. While these may be productive results for many congregations, they are not adequate criteria for judging the effectiveness of a church.

The congregation is a corporate body under the laws of the state but a community of believers in actual purpose. It behaves as a voluntary organization according to some management types, but it has a spiritual inclination different from any other voluntary group. Since it is different from other groups, its management must reflect not only this difference but also the purpose for which the church is established.

We have discussed the congregation's responsibility to be a steward of its resources. This is an attitude important for congregations to assume if they want realistically to implement their plans. This same attitude ought to be used in any managing done by pastors or lay leaders during program development, implementation, and administration. The stewardship focus of a manager is on caring, appreciation, and willingness to allow some inefficiency if that helps accomplish the goals and purposes of the congregation while helping individuals meet some of their personal religious goals.

Effective managing is being careful with resources and making certain that resources are used to produce desired results. Being a steward doesn't mean that a pastor or lay person functions without skills or is not disciplined. Rather it means that each must be in tune with the spiritual nature and intent of the congregation.

What are some signs of a manager being a steward? They include at least the following.

1. A continuing emphasis will be upon training and education. Committees, organizations, and administrative activities involve groups of people. They are task oriented, they want to accomplish something. They need to be told over and over again that their activities are to achieve the purposes of the congregation, that their deliberations as a body of believers may include honest disagreement, that they will have to negotiate and compromise as they map out a plan of action, and that their primary task is to witness to Christ through the congregation's programs. Managing as a steward emphasizes education.

2. Careful use of and cultivation of people resources indicates a manager as a steward. This doesn't mean being a Scrooge or a willy-nilly administrator. It signifies a sensitivity to the needs and capabilities of people and a desire to help them find their best niche to work as a part of the congregation's corps of volunteers. People are treated well. They are recruited as a normal part of the weekly activities of the pastor and church leaders.

3. Managers who are also stewards demonstrate stewardship in their management of money and facilities. This is discussed in detail in chapter 5.

4. The corporate worship experience is not a time for showing off individual talents or skills but a time to use them for the glory of God. Nothing in the planning or execution of a worship service should be routine or perfunctory. The order of worship, hymns, and prayers may be familiar but nothing should be treated as old hat.

Managing as a steward affects the entire set of activities of a congregation. Results are expected, goals are to be met, fiscal responsibility is essential, and volunteers are to be recruited.

The difference between managing as a steward and managing in the business motif is the motivation behind it. Realism in the congregation requires a sense of stewardship in management which pushes toward achieving purposes and goals.

Before the Crisis

Planning is supposed to help congregations be in control of at least part of their future. Inadvertent errors or oversights can snowball into crises with great speed. Just because a plan is developed and is being implemented does not mean the congregation is immune from crises.

The emphases on communication and alerting people to needs and opportunities, the central calendar as a checkpoint for all programs, and the management of the congregation within the parameters of stewardship are important ways of preventing crises. These techniques can smooth out the daily living of a congregation so that its conflicts and disagreements may not grow unchecked into major confrontations.

How decisions are made is another factor in preventing crises. The stress upon putting a plan together, negotiating, and being realistic in implementation strategies assumes a process in which decisions are made and agreed on by both the governing body and the congregation (when appropriate). Unfortunately, life isn't as smooth or as rational as it's made to appear.

People have strong opinions, they have bad days and years, they have dislikes and preferences, and they feel superior or threatened. People can be helpful or they can be disruptive. In the illustration of the women's group and the senior citizens' program date conflict, this conflict could easily have resulted in a major confrontation. It didn't because the pastor acted swiftly and kept the issue on a nonthreatening base. Both sides came out as winners. This often can be done but there are times when nothing seems to work. At such times, giving people time to think and calm down seems to be the only solution.

Let's consider some ways to ensure that decision making will result in crisis prevention.

1. Decisions ought to be made well in advance. For example, previous discussions in this book have indicated that the planning process has several kinds of decision points included in addition to those involved in planning new programs. Who's

in charge of communication, where the responsibilities for immediate decision making lie, training processes which can motivate or reassign volunteers, handling money and facilities, and evaluating are some of the places where the planning committee sets in motion processes for making decisions.

Decisions which are made in advance and without the heat of emotion can be referred to later as the points for further negotiation or refinement. If decisions are not made early, the possibility of a later crisis is great.

2. Designated committees and persons should be responsible for particular types of decisions. The responsibilities of each committee include making decisions appropriate to the committee's programming. They should make those decisions and keep themselves out of the business of other groups. For example, a worship committee can decide upon the hymnals to be used by a congregation. It may also try to find out the kinds of hymns which are most familiar to the congregation. However, it is not the worship committee's business to choose the specific hymns for a worship service. This is the task of the pastor or music director. To step outside the bounds of clear responsibility is to create a crisis.

3. An emergency decision-making procedure should be established. The pastor with the problem of getting money for a youth program, in the example cited, used an established emergency decision-making procedure. It had been set up by the planning committee and affirmed by the governing body.

Every organization is going to have emergencies so it makes good sense to establish a procedure to handle them. The procedure describes who should call the group together, what limits there are on the kinds of decisions that can be made by whom, how approval of the decisions can be obtained, and how to fund emergency decisions.

4. A person who will be responsible for resolving potential conflicts should be identified. In the case of the two groups with the same date for their events, the pastor acted as the arbitrator. The pastor may have this function in most congregations for most issues. A secretary who keeps the calendar may be assigned the duty of alerting people to possible conflicts in dates in order to reduce the need for arbitration. However, someone should be assigned the task of making certain any potential conflict over

dates or priority claims is cleared up before it can become a crisis.

5. The planning committee or the governing body should retain the responsibility for approving all decisions which affect the implementation of the programs of the congregation. The approval is not complicated in most cases and may be based on the recommendation of the pastor or other church leader. In some cases, however, the approval may need discussion time at a regularly scheduled meeting. In a few instances a decision by the governing body will be required since the tentative decision in a conflict of priorities was to defer to the governing body. In the final analysis, the governing body must make the binding decisions regarding congregational programs.

These suggestions are based on the premise that decisions made prior to a conflict by the governing body of the congregation will prevent many crises. When a crisis does occur, the mechanism for decision making should have been established so that it can be used to limit the crisis period. Things don't always work the way we would like them to, but planning to prevent crises will make life much easier when priorities seem to conflict.

Rationality, Not Panic

The unknown, the new, the strange, and the unexpected often create exaggerated fears. Horror films take advantage of this tendency by using sudden and strange film effects to play tricks on our imagination. The producers know that the technique of suggestion works and their purpose is fulfilled.

Few congregations have to face horror films as reality, although fire, theft, and vandalism are experiences which many must live through. These are horrors in that they are unexpected, cause much pain, and represent financial and emotional costs. The chain of reactions to these kinds of events includes anger, followed by sorrow, followed by frustration. The conviction to do something constructive is usually reached after a person or the leadership of a congregation has experienced all of these emotions.

It is at the point of doing something constructive that rationality begins to take over. Being able to return to a plan or to follow an emergency procedure enables a person once again to be in control of a situation. No matter if the event which precipitates potential panic is as dramatic as a fire or as mundane as discovering a conflict of dates for two important groups in the church, the need is not to panic but to be in control of the situation. The planning process can help with this but it is not a guarantee that rationality will be used. A plan is only as rational as the people who use it.

Suppose a crisis develops in the congregation. Who handles it? What is the decision-making process for emergencies? How involved is the total membership? Where is money kept for immediate and emergency use? Who has the authority to speak for the congregation?

These questions, when anticipated, can be used to develop a plan for maintaining rationality during times which scream for panic. It isn't necessary to outline the procedures to be used for every possible catastrophe which can befall a congregation. What is essential is a general plan of dealing with any contingency. (The development of the contingency plan was discussed in chapter 4.) The point to be made now is that the leadership must be ready to rely on those procedures as guidelines for dealing with a crisis.

As with most other parts of bringing realism into a plan, substituting rationality for panic depends on the attitudes and actions of the congregation's leaders. They must be convinced of the purpose and nature of their congregation and be willing to move carefully to meet its goals and purposes. As a group, they will meet quickly following the unforeseen crisis and handle it. They will then explain to the congregation the circumstances, the content of their deliberations, and the method they feel will best deal with the problem.

This procedure can be used with events as diverse as a fire, the rupture of a water heater, two groups choosing the same date to hold a major event, or the sudden illness of a pastor. In each instance the group which has been designated to be in charge of emergencies for that program will meet and design a plan of action. This group will designate a spokesperson to present the plan to the congregation and to indicate how the revised program is to be implemented.

Panic is a debilitating emotion. It causes people and congregations to do strange things. The best thing about it is that it is avoidable. Making certain a procedure is in place which can handle emergencies goes a long way to curb panic. That procedure should be part of every plan.

Remember the Purpose

One of the rallying cries many elementary school children read about was "Remember the Alamo," referring to the Texas fort which became a symbol in a war with Mexico. In this book the continual emphasis upon remembering the purposes of your congregation may be the singular rallying cry. At no time does a congregation which is implementing its plan lose sight of its purposes.

A continuing concern of ministers is that programs and planning reflect a theology of the church. That's true but it's clergy language. "Purpose" is a lay term which includes theology but suggests a more active approach to planning. Purpose implies that someone is supposed to do something about achieving it. On the other hand a theological statement, by its nature, is foundational and can be viewed as a passive pronouncement.

Most planning processes begin by creating a statement of purpose and theology. This is the base upon which programs are built and witnessing proceeds. A plan without a purpose is useless. A purpose without an underlying theology is not helpful. In the best planning document the purpose with its underlying theology will be spelled out. In most plans the purpose *assumes* a theology of the church. It would be better to make the theology explicit.

The purpose has to be clear and concise. It is the building block upon which all the goals and programs rest. It must be recalled continually so that members of the community of believers are aware of their potential as well as of their responsibilities as witnesses to the fact of Christ. Being realistic requires a basis for action. That's called the purpose. It has to be remembered at all times by all members of the congregation if they want to implement their plan.

Realism in planning requires commitment to make a plan succeed. The techniques and attitudes discussed in this book can help achieve realism and implement plans. It is up to the pastors, leaders, and members of congregations, however, to determine how committed they are to achieving their purpose as people witnessing to Jesus Christ. Only then can they become the proclaimers that a realistic plan intends them to be.

References for Further Study

The following is a selected list of books which deal with topics in this book.

Anderson, J. D., and Jones, Ezra Earl, *The Management of Ministry*, San Francisco: Harper & Row, Publishers Inc., 1978.

Benn, Alec, *The Twenty-seven Most Common Mistakes in Advertising*, New York: Amacom, 1978.

Burnett, Joseph D., *Capital Funds Campaign Manual for Churches*, Valley Forge: Judson Press, 1980.

Dayton, Edward R., and Engstrom, Ted W., *Strategy for Leadership*, Old Tappan: New Jersey: Fleming H. Revell Co., 1979.

DeBoer, John, *Let's Plan*, New York: The Pilgrim Press, 1970.

Dudley, Carl S., *Where Have All Our People Gone?*, New York: The Pilgrim Press, 1979.

Drucker, Peter F., *The Practice of Management*, New York: Harper & Row, Publishers, Inc., 1954.

Ellis, Loudell O., *Church Treasurer's Handbook*, Valley Forge: Judson Press, 1978.

Lingren, Alvin J., and Shawchuck, Norman, *Management for Your Church*, Nashville: Abingdon Press, 1977.

McLeod, Thomas E., *The Work of the Church Treasurer*, Valley Forge: Judson Press, 1981.

Middleton, Robert G., *Charting a Course for the Church*, Valley Forge: Judson Press, 1979.

Rusbuldt, Richard E., Gladden, Richard K., and Green, Norman M., Jr., *Key Steps in Local Church Planning,* Valley Forge: Judson Press, 1980.

Rusbuldt, Richard E., Gladden, Richard K., and Green, Norman M., Jr., *Local Church Planning Manual,* Valley Forge: Judson Press, 1977.

Schaller, Lyle E., *Effective Church Planning,* Nashville: Abingdon Press, 1979.

Southard, Samuel, *Religious Inquiry,* Nashville: Abingdon Press, 1976.

White, Robert N., editor, *Managing Today's Church,* Valley Forge: Judson Press, 1981.